D1759905

insidepoetry
Voices from prison

Inside Poetry is produced on a 'not for profit' basis.
Copies are donated to all UK prison libraries.
Additional copies are available for sale
via our website: www.insidtime.org

VOLUME 6

Edited by Rachel Billington

First published in 2014 by Inside Time Ltd

Inside Time, Botley Mills, Botley, Southampton, Hampshire SO30 2GB.
Telephone: 0844 335 6483
www.insidetime.org

Inside Time is a 'not for profit' organisation

ISBN 978-0-9927408-1-8

Layout by Tonic Design - info@tonicdesign.net
Printed and bound by CPI Group (UK) Ltd, Croydon, CR0 4YY

Cover image: Untitled 1, HMP Peterborough, collage on board.
Caro Millington Highly Commended Award for Mixed Media.
Image courtesy of the Koestler Trust.

"These poems are sad and honest and true, and they will strike a chord with all kinds of people whose captivity may be mental rather than physical. Well done Inside Time, and let's hope this volume inspires such a spirit of creative competition in our prisons that someone somewhere produces the next Ballad of Reading Gaol".

Boris Johnson - *Mayor of London (about Volume 1)*

"I hear so much when I read these poems. Clearly those who wrote them have much to say and the poems have unlocked thoughts and feelings which might otherwise have remained hidden and suppressed. This is poetry at its most effective, enabling people to find a voice, to say what they might not have dared to say so openly before. Though their authors might remain locked up, at least for a while, their feelings have been freed. They have a life of their own now and their message can reach anyone with eyes to read and ears to hear".

Michael Palin - *Author, traveller and humorist (about Volume 1)*

"To read this anthology (referring to Volume 2) is to be taken to the heart and soul of the prison system in this country and to take the living pulses of its inmates. Individually, the poems offer up single voices; but cumulatively they become a huge, human, hurting chorus that we should all listen to with the greatest of attention and humility. To take up a pen and begin to express oneself in a poem is, in itself, an act of giving and of sharing".

Carole Ann Duffy - *Poet Laureate (about Volume 2)*

"Readers will find funny poems, sad poems, introspective poems, world-wise poems - poems, in fact, which fit and realise every mood under the sun and moon. For all these reasons, the anthology is a deeply enjoyable one. Its exceptional value lies in the fact that it releases and validates the voices it contains".

Andrew Motion - *Poet Laureate 1999-2009 (about Volume 1)*

"Anyone looking for an authentic flavour of what prison life really means for those who have to live it need look no further than this powerful new collection from Inside Time. Normally hidden from the world and each other - the pieces in this book reveal the most private thoughts and feelings of the people who make up the incarcerated community across our penal estate. Within these pages are cries full of hurt, laughter, rage and hope and all deserve to be heard".

Erwin James - *Writer and ex-prisoner* *(about Volume 2)*

"As we struggle to make sense of whatever world we find around us, two of our most important supports are rhythm and form. We are pattern-making creatures. The voices in this book are responding to a world most of us never see, but which reflects, nevertheless, the whole human condition. Through engaging with craft, these thoughtful and honest writers show us that even in our darkest times - under "razor wire skies," as one of them puts it - poetry can fulfil one of humanity's deepest needs: to express what is within, to let the bird out of the cage".

Ruth Padel - *Poet (about Volume 3)*

"That they are written by prisoners makes these poems worthy of note, but what makes them enjoyable, what makes them intense, what makes them in many instances profound and moving is that they are written by human beings - human beings who suffer and laugh, and who love and hate. You may pick this volume up thinking of it as just a curiosity, but I guarantee that as you read the poems they will draw you in until you are fully in the condition of those who have written them - until you, too, are visited with an uncalled for isolation".

Will Self - *Novelist & broadcaster (about Volume 2)*

Introduction

Incarceration is a terrible thing but it also can give time for reflection. Often our contributors are writing down their innermost feelings, the shame, fear, anger, love and hope, for the very first time. Poetry offers them a means of expression which they have never found before. This gives each poem a rawness and truth which a more professional poet may strive to achieve.

Over the six years we have published poetry in Inside Time, followed each year by a collected volume, Chloe and I who read them recognise the voice of certain men and women (always more men than women to reflect the percentages in prison) who are growing not only in self knowledge but also in imaginative creativity.

Included in this collection are many different kinds of poetry; the autobiographical or story poem is always strongly represented as is the love poem addressed in thanks to a lover, a mother or child. Drugs and anger are cause of bitter self reproach while prison food, petty prison rules and politicians unfairness evoke a satiric reaction. It is unfortunate for Minister of Justice, Chris Grayling, that his name rhymes with 'failing'.

A reader with little knowledge of prisons would learn a lot from reading this collection. Indeed one of our aims in publishing this book is to give the prisoner a voice outside the barbed wire and high walls. As always we will give one free copy of Inside Poetry Volume 6 to each prison library and also a discount to those who buy through Inside Time. The book is also available through high street bookshops and online book suppliers.

These poems are only a small proportion of those sent to Inside Time every day of the year. Going public with a personal poem demands a level of bravery. The accompanying letters suggest that the act of writing a poem brings a little light into the dark and tangled maze of the prison experience.

Rachel Billington
Editor

CONTENTS

Stuck In A Rut

This prison predicament, it's just a blip
I'll soon be back with some cash on my hip
No more baggage, free to roam
Wherever I kick off my shoes will be home
Jump on a plane with a bag on my back
Looking for adventure off the beaten track
I could base jump into the Grand Canyon or white water raft
Or roller blade the Great Wall of China, naked, just for a laugh
Or scuba dive the Great Barrier Reef and swim with sharks
Or trek the Inca Trail to Machu Picchu backwards so I'd end up at the start
Get lost in the Amazon rainforest with no compass or machete
Ride wildebeest bareback in the vast Serengeti
But for tonight when I kick off these shoes and the door slams shut
Today's adventure is over; I'm back in the cell, stuck in a rut.

AA HMP Northumberland

Time Chamber

Preserved in my time chamber
Just one, myself and I the Lone Ranger
No friends, enemies or strangers
Preserved in my time chamber
Safety without danger
Time doesn't fly it drags in my time chamber
But I age slow, I feel like a teenager
Preserved in my time chamber
Staying busy is a no brainer
Read, write, study, plan while I'm preserved in my time chamber
Pray, exercise, meditate in my time chamber
My time chamber is a changer
I'm doing things I've never done before so I'm greater
Adversity's a great motivator
Preserved in my time chamber
No TV just a radio and pen and paper
Books, magazines, newspapers in my time chamber
I'm doing it my way in my time chamber
But I cope, I have hopes and I'm a high aimer
Reach for the stars when I get out of my time chamber
I've been preserved feel my energy surge later
For now I'm submerged deep in patience in a chamber of time
This place of mine
Where I pay for my crime
My time chamber

Adetoye Adeniyi HMP Garth

Inside Out

Vertical shadows on the wall
Fence outside, straight and tall
Footsteps on the steel floor
Someone peeps through the door

Steel gates clang, voices heard
I must admit I do feel scared
Guilt is here, gone is pride
My mind's in here, my hearts outside

The long night's gone, it's breakfast time
The cells are opened, we stand in line
Back to my pad, food on a tray
I sit and wonder what happens today

The tannoy goes off, it echoes about
What they say, I can't make out
Is it induction? Education? I don't know
Whatever it is, be ready to go

The day goes by, lunch and tea
But still no job, or education for me
Recreation is good - and exercise
Gives me the chance to walk off the pies
The best thing for me is on the phone
The nearest thing to being at home

I phone my lady who I love dear
And after the call I shed a tear
After a shower and a chat to the lads
We're all banged up again in our pads

I'll read a book or watch TV
And think of the places I'd like to be
The night has come and darkness falls
Back to the vertical shadows on the wall

AG HMP Whatton

Daddy Has Gone

How do you sit down and talk to your son and tell
Him that his daddy has gone
Its easier explaining the meaning of death and
Why people die and draw their last breath

But daddy, he's gone to no peaceful heaven
Instead he's in prison and serving seven
So how do you sit down and tell you own son
The whys and the reasons his daddy has gone?

Listen my son, you'll need to be strong
Daddy has done something terribly wrong
He's gone into prison for quite a long time
And this is what happens when you commit crime

Daddy still loves us, he'll phone and he'll write
Ring you to wish you goodnight and sleep tight
We can sit down together and write him a letter
It'll make daddy smile and make him feel better

We can go and see daddy perhaps once a week
To give him a hug and a kiss on the cheek
You can draw daddy pictures and paintings at school
To put on his wall which will look really cool

I tried telling my son with emotional tact
The truth of the matter, you can't hide the fact
His daddy has gone and has gone for a while
You can't say it with flowers or manage a smile

So how do you sit down and talk to your son
And answer his questions why daddy has gone
All you can do is just tell him your way
And tell him daddy will be home one day

Jared Ainsworth HMP Swinfen Hall

C.S.U Unit

Locked up in C.S.U
24 hours with nothing to see
Four weeks and deemed dangerous
Not fit for normal location
Years and years of pain deep inside
Angry at how the system perceives me
Even the D.S.P.D couldn't help me
Everything is bleak, the clouds dark
Deep inside my thoughts are hard
Labelled with a personality disorder
Impulsive, angry/violent, I kind of agree
But now I'm lost within a system
Where hospital or C.S.C looms
The end of the road, God help me
I cry with tears, have feelings
A life sentence, many years inside
Psychiatrists, psychologist say "damaged", "we're sorry"
Hoping for the right help/intervention
I pray for this for a right direction

Anon HMP Whitemoor

Like The Sinking Ship I Go Down

The proverbial rats don't hang around
I start with a paddle and cling onto the raft
Education is drowning I need to graft
A lifeguard, a mentor
A prison guard a preventer
Take a deep breath, go under again
It's hard to get back up for air
To learn, to breathe from depths of despair
Throw me a line, get me aboard
Infinite wisdom lost on F.N.C...Bored
Like the sinking ship I go down
Inspiration a dying ember
As February turns to September
Just to become a better person
As the alternatives only to worsen
To builds self esteem learn respect
Without access to education what do they expect?
A prison without a success rate
Is the prison that failed to educate
Is the government really to blame?
Or the prison system playing a game?

Anon HMP Preston

Lord Loquacious

I will wax lyrical in my persuasive voice
Being captivated is your only choice.
Gather round and experience the latest hit
But avoid being drenched by my flying spit.

Hail the self-appointed Lord Loquacious
Who will legitimise the outrageous?
Let's discuss snow leopards and banker's greed
I guarantee both your ears will bleed.

I'm the pun prince and the king of quip.
Beware my tongue is as sharp as a whip.
No need for hustings or a soapbox,
In 'Speakers Corner no one will out fox.

You're listening to Lord Loquacious,
Never mundane, always audacious.
I will talk specific or the Atlantic
In shades of grey or crazy frantic.

When talking sport there's no opinion but mine,
Tapping my watch I insist on Fergie time.
Referees and umpires we should savour,
Then send the useless bunch to Spec-Savers.

Pay attention to your Lord Loquacious,
Nowt between the ears but my headroom's spacious.
When I ruminate about austerity and Iraq,
Only the depth varies as we wallow in crap.

Do we want Liz or the Duke of Hazard?
I'd rather be represented by Eddie Izzard.
We need to replace the head on the stamp,
With the marathon man, the queen of camp.

These are the words of Lord Loquacious,
Fickle in attitude, sanity suspicious.
No time for authority and I never conform,
I'm the melting icecaps and Desert Storm.

Life's a gas or it will be with fracking,
Earthquakes are what Britain's really lacking.
Fighting the War on Terror is so yesterday,
Return our civil rights and our freedom, we say.

Continued ...

Stand to admire your Lord Loquacious.
I maybe rash but it isn't contagious.
Remember your well-being, so don't be amiss,
Stay fit by avoiding the National Health Service.

Let's machinate about our tired democracy.
Two parties with their heads in the lavatories.
Vote Sergeant Pepper or the Raving Loons,
They won't tax your extra bedrooms.

Fear not Lord Loquacious has the stage,
My words of wisdom are all the rage.
Revolution I teach, changes I'll bring,
Seasonally adjusted, our Arab spring.

Citizens let's start our bloodless coup,
Governments and juntas your days are through.
We need a head of state that is gracious,
Time to promote the unassuming Lord Loquacious.

Anon

Mouse

When I was young there was a maid
She was shy and quiet and seemed afraid
She worked in my family's house
Scurried fast and silent, just like a mouse
When she was working she had no voice, no sound
When I was a child she was always around
She was happy to chat with me and to play
So long as men would keep away
In my house she was treated well
But there was something she was unwilling to tell
The children would listen when she would call
But to others she hardly spoke at all
Small like the lavender tree, picturesque was she
Others looked at her as a servant, but she was a friend to me

Anon HMP Low Moss

Love Or Life

I've sent you a thousand letters
I've phone you a hundred times
I've sent you countless VO's
But still you don't reply
You said you'd always be there
But now you can't be seen
You've left me high and dry
In my time of need
I know I broke the law
Now I'm doing time
But it's time I'm paying twice
If you're no longer mine

I could do twenty years
If you were by my side
But six months without your love
Might as well be life

AS HMP Oakwood

Plagiarism

It's no surprise
That some plagiarise
In other words steal or loan
But realise
If you want the prize
Write rhymes that are your own
Don't be one of those
Who gets exposed
In the pages of Inside Time
Coz you're a fool
If you break that rule
Coz plagiarism is a crime

AS HMP Oakwood

I Was Just A Young Man

I was just a young man
Searching for some answers
Looked up to Biggie, Dre and other gangsters
2Pac Shakur
RIP it was your music that inspired me
I seen no changes
But then I had a reason
As I heard a heart beat
Then I seen you breathing
You are daddy's number one
I think I've found my answer
I'd rather be a perfect dad
Rather than a gangster

George Banister HMP Durham

Suicide In Prison

I knew a classic prison boy
Who smiled at time in hollow joy
In between reading books
He'd whistle, to feed the ducks

In the dungeon, full of fear
Boils, cockroaches and strapped for beer
He placed the noose round his head
In the morning he was dead

Terry Barrass HMP Moorland

Happily Never After

You're much too good for me my petal
You can do so much better, why settle?
This is just the way that things should end
Don't worry I'll always be your friend
I would follow you to the world's end
But you're too good for this life, no need to pretend
Plus your family will never accept me
All their ever gonna do is reject me
To be fair, they can't be blamed
Looking at me like a jail boy that can't be tamed
You will always be special to me
It's a shame I can't provide the stability
That's needed to settle down in a family
I'm doubting that jail will make a man of me
But I'd love to think we'd end up together
But you'll leave me in your past if you're clever
Coz I don't act like a Mr, I act like a Master
And all I do ends up in disaster
Even though we could have fun times filled with laughter
I don't think I can be your happily ever after

Michael Bateman HMP Channings Woods

Once I Thought

Once I laughed at believers
Called them deluded and deceived
Once I thought them fools in blinkers
Unable to see the facts that I perceived

I saw nothing that I wanted
In religions or their holy creeds
God for me was just an idea
Far too distant to ever meet my needs

When I heard of the hate and cruelty
Of the faithful with their bloodied hands
All I saw was the dismal failure
Of all those different Godly brands

All those roads that led to heaven
Couldn't any of them be true
All those ways were far too narrow
None fit for me to pass through

Then there came the time of trial
A fall into a pit of deep despair
I committed an act of utter madness
An evil that I can never repair

Who will ever forgive my sin
If I cannot forgive myself
Who will stand by my side
If I have thrown away life's true wealth

I realise now that all my choices
Have been made with myself in mind
A life full of wrong turnings
Lived in the country of the blind

But now I see the true meaning
Of those words I used to scorn
Now I see it's time I was living
The life God meant for me when I was born

What a friend I have in Jesus
If for me he made his sacrifice
What a love he does show me
If he paid that ultimate price

Continued ...

Who can say I'm not forgiven
When I repent with all my heart
Who can say that I'm not chosen
When the love he gives sets none apart

I may never regain what I have lost
But I can never lose what now I've gained
For now at last I have the freedom
To forever live a life unchained

Robert Beck HMP Grendon

I Didn't Know

I didn't know I was poor
I lived in a hut next to the beach
Swam in the deep blue sea
In old jeans cut into shorts
Walked the beach with sand between my toes
Picked coconut, pineapple and bananas only when hungry
My skin getting darker and darker as days in sun became weeks
I didn't know I was poor until a little American girl
In her Gucci sun glasses and swimwear said...
"Look at the poor white man; can I give him some money Mommy?"

Johan Berg HMP Bure

Stop Snoring

Stop snoring
Here we are again
In a twelve foot box
With a pad and a pen
A cell mate who snores
I'm in prison again
I'm sick of the yard
And I'm sick of the fence
Where do I keep going wrong?
And who in this jail has the answer?
Probation... NOMS
Or whatever they call it
The call of the courses
That I keep ignoring
All the reports
And all of the scoring
I find them intrusive
And mentally boring
The only person with the answer is me
I know what I've done
I've seen what I've seen
If I'm going to stop
Then it's all down to me
I'll unlock the door
With the key to my dreams
Truth is that I've got a problem
And right now it's snoring
Should I unlock the door to probation
And open my mind to their courses
Help them to score
And to fill out reports
Is it my life that I've been ignoring?
I'm locked up in prison
My life I am missing
No woman to love
With no hugging and kissing
I ain't got a job
And I ain't got a vision
I'm wasting my talents
In life that I'm living
Cannot go shopping
Cannot go fishing
Cannot go clubbing
Cannot go flirting
Is this the life

Continued ...

And how I should live it
Somehow I doubt it
Now I am thinking
Give in to probation
Give into their courses
Open my mind
To their thoughts and reporting
Give them a chance
Even if they are boring
Why?
Coz I'm sick of my cell mate
And sick of his snoring

Liam Blackmore HMP Cardiff

Life, IPP, EPP, Recall

When will I get out
No one seems to know
'Conduct yourself in the right way man
And then we'll let you know
It's our show
We decide who goes on set
Then we'll decide what you get'
I think there is a word for that
I think that word is pet
I bet
It's my life
You may fight me for it
But I won't let you take it
And if I cannot really change
Then I'll bloody fake it
I'll fake it and you all can say
'That's guys done good
Let him play
I say
Our system works a treat'
I think this is a repeat
I've seen this one before
I know how it ends
Now just open up the door
No more
Why can't they just see
I only want to be free

Darel Blackrose HMP Stocken

Lovers Lips

Lover's lips await outside
Even given choice
Chance and time and
Moment brief
Little but a voice
Heard in darkness
Seen in light
Wanting all the more
To walk the streets
To step outside
To place my hand in yours

Thomas Boord-James HMP Wayland

Poor Ant

Tiny ant so clever and strong
Come under my door singing his song
Looking left then checking right
He makes his dash in cover of night
Fast as he can his little legs tore
His heart was racing as the big giant snore
Looking for sugar or anything sweet
The giant stirs and lumbers to his feet
Normally quick the little ant run
He didn't have a chance his life had just begun
How guilty I felt his life so ended
As he lay on the floor twisted and bended
Did he have family waiting at home
Brothers and sisters
The queen on her throne
Now every night by the door
There's a sprinkle of sugar placed on the floor
So those little ants come by late
They can eat in peace
And not suffer the same fate

Stephen Boorman Prison Supplied

N Wing

I sit in my pad locked up for the night
We're locked up early because of a fight
Double bubble is always the cause
Two subbied inmates with grey open pores

I wonder why they take all that stuff
Or make a deal we all know is duff
There's nothing new it's always the same
Like a cold dark day with drizzly rain

It's a working wing so we are out in the day
Time goes quicker we like it that way
People joke and pretend they are friends
They are just killing time and working for spends

Tuesday is canteen, the wing is all calm
Debtors pay up or face bodily harm
You know who they are when the big men arrive
They rush in a cell like bees to a hive

Nobody sees or hears the noise
The big men leave with calm and poise
Friends follow in talking the big
If they had been there they would have a dig

Nobody cares, the screws hide away
Has this become my normal day?
We sit in our cages completely forgotten
Waiting to appease a system that's rotten

Peter Bradley HMP Birmingham

Scottish Slang - Kit (Heroin)

Try some Kit see wit a kin do
I've killed more people than World War 2
I'll make your life pure pain an hell
Your Maw's your Da's bros an sisters as well
You might start aff at once a week
I'll get ya high take yae to your peak
Then you'll want tae try some more
Before you know, you're kicking in a door
Grab that telly, video anaw
Rob yir granny, con yir maw
Now nothing will stand in your way
You need me now everyday
You thought you were strong and ready to fight this battle
But you've no git me you'll start tae rattle
Now everything you're about is greed
I've got a plan for you. a want you deed
I targeted you at your lowest level
You know who sent me, your pal the devil
So gee some tae your mate as well
I'll keep your seat warm in hell

Gary Braiden HMP Addiewell

In Line

You sob for Saturday's sins bleakly
And like a perforated edge; line up weakly
The brave front you cling too tight
Is confiscated on the first night

The evening previous; a girl beside
You wait to enter the club, music blares out
Neon lights bounce above glistening filmy faces
Weaves wild shapes and scraps for spaces

Lining up interned, agitated and alone
Prise contacts from memory, a brief call
Russian doll blues, tears inside of tears
Boxed-in fears, stacked tier upon tier

Bodies twist, writhing en masse
A banging night out - on the lash
Green beams locked on dilated stares
Little loves lost; plenty shared

The wing flaps and they all fall out
"Bang up in five minutes", they shout
An ice cold shower, left wet through
Corralled into your coop; one last queue

That gawper's gaze, flipped jealous rage
Fuse lit quick, wick lost in the mix
You hastily mistook an innocent look
A loss of control left two souls broken

Snatching sleep; you're far from fine
Back-logged, slumber soon piles up
You wait in line, a final time
Dreams stuck, laying lost and out of luck

Matthew Bramhall HMP Preston

Sorry State

Stand fast; roll check
No exercise because it's wet
Dinner's late and canteen's short
Answer back and you're on report
The inability to count, is no excuse
They wonder why all the abuse
Blame unto others: "DHL were late"
Simply said; a sorry state

Thirty cons to just one screw
Gleaming routine: brand new
Practice runs put in place
Still we wander around in space
Bursting jails house cramped minds
Hemmed in by scruffy rules; it stinks inside
The west is the best, they propagate
Simply said; a sorry state

Learned eyes should look and see
The disparity of the I.E.P
Underprivileged with no incentives
So try again, but be inventive

Basic through to Standard
The gap gapes quite far
Earn trust and work hard
But still seem, stuck at the start
Standard up to Enhanced
Isn't much of an advance?
All it does is infuriate
Simply said; a sorry state

Matthew Bramhall HMP Preston

Prison Issue

Prison issue boxers
And prison issue socks
Prison issue shoes
'cos yours were taken by the cops

Prison issue coffee sachets
Freeze-dried, weak and bitter
Pour a cup, take a sip
...then flush it down the shitter

Prison issue toothpaste
Squeezed into pea-sized balls
Used for sticking NUTS girls
To your prison issue walls

Prison issue tea bags
Doubled up for extra taste
You tried them once, you won't again
...more prison issue waste

Prison issue shampoo
And prison issue soap
Makes a weighty line
Tied on your prison bed sheet rope

Prison issue toiletries
Will never keep you clean
F**k this prison issue shit
And bring on my canteen!

Mr Brand HMP Bristol

Bully Boy

In prison you will meet them all
Some are big, and some are small
Although, everywhere you go, you will meet a 'Bully Boy'
The kind that intimidates and uses you as their toy
They will do it to you in all kinds of ways
And do to you, on most of the days
It can be done with a violence or come from the mouth
Draining your emotions and sending your bottom lip south
If you think you can tell on them, you become a grass
Then you will find, the 'Bully Boys' come in mass
So what do you do when you meet your 'Bully Boy'?
Do you hurt yourself, grass or become their toy?
Do you let them hurt you or rob all your canteen?
Let the others join in and become the victim machine?
'No' Mr 'Bully Boy', you will not be bullying me today
Coz I'm not your victim for you to play!
I'll stand my ground and show how weak you really are
I'll slash your face and leave a nasty scar
Maybe "I'll" get "my" mates and we rush "you" in the shower
Leave "you" bleeding and start flexing "my" power?
It's not like I can grass or show my weakness
So I become stronger and lose all my sweetness
I'll fight back and hurt you and maybe all your mates
Soon it will be "you" paying all the canteen rates
So now I live large and you have become "my toy"
And the sadness sinks in, as I realise I'm the "Bully Boy"

Brooksy HMP Leicester

Monotonous Confinement

No hellos, no goodbyes
No good morning, no goodnight
No how are you? How was your day?
All alone, what can I say?

Lonely days, lonely nights
Past and present, dark and light
Good and evil, wrong and right
Worry for my mental psyche

Who are you? Who am I?
Can you hear me when I sigh?
Was I here? Was I there?
I am here in my chair

Did I give? Did I steal?
No more life, just a turning wheel
Do I laugh? Or should I cry?
Oh how I miss my family life

Does it matter who I am?
Can another understand?
Was I young? Am I old?
There are too many truths untold

Can you see me in my chair?
Am I here? Are you there?
Break the silence let out a scream
Talk to the enemy, or is it a dream?

Here I sit alone in my chair
I cannot breath there is no air
I know that things didn't go well
This is the monotony in a prison cell

Dominic Browne HMP Dumfries

A Momentary Lapse Of Reality

A hedgehog spoke to a parrot
Who spoke to a tree
The tree spoke to the wind
Who then whispered to me

I told the wind
To tell the tree
Who told the parrot
To tell the hedgehog
To speak to me

The hedgehog told the parrot
To tell the tree
Who told the wind
To whisper to me

So I met the hedgehog
On the grassy knoll
For me to find out
I don't speak hedgehog

Gordon Burgess HMP Isle of Wight

My Only True Friend

You don't listen to me
I talk to you
And you talk to me
But you just don't listen

You show me things
That have no real meaning
You show me joy and wonder
Laughter and fear

I scream and shout
I answer most of your questions
I even get some right
You are my love, my only true friend

So why am I ignored
Oh why don't you listen
Do you love me
Do you really care

I do everything for you
I turn you on
Turn you over
Make sure you're clean

Oh I think I've worked it out
I bet I know the answer
Is it because
You're my TV

Gordon Burgess HMP Isle of Wight

The Lion And Me

Why does the lion pace his
Cage like I do? is he
Like me looking for a way
Out and never finding it
Is it a deep seeded
Instinctive drive to stay
Fit and active. Is
He like me imagining
He's on open expanse
Of grass with no restricting
Walls chaining his animal
Spirit. Is it simple because
There is nothing else to do
Other than walk until he sleeps
Or is it him trying to avoid
The maddening troubles
Outside these crazed
Walls. I wonder if
The lion paces his cage
And ponders why I pace
Back and forwards continuously

Tony Bushby HMP Aylesbury

The Suicide

You get them all in here, the sad, the mad and the bad
Best look out for them but not for reasons that'd make you glad
The sad you look out for with different eyes
The boys don't go in for very long goodbyes

The sad have a con, they like to fill you with laughter
Side step you with tales of a happy ever after
Not too much, no telling of the joys life has brought
Just enough to curve you from their one true thought

Some people use prison to re-boot and kick start
Others more obsessed with holding on to affairs of the heart
The opportunist is more circumspect, planning a new first
The sad just find reasons for thinking the worst

I didn't know the latest guy to jump from here to there
That long dark fall from the demons he could not bear
Maybe even sleep would only mess with his head
Dreams fractured by monsters cursing his bed

So there he flees into the great secret he now knows
Floating off to mysterious, spirit suffering no more blows
It's over for this lad, but I didn't catch his name
I can guess why he left, I didn't know him, but I've felt his pain

Don't worry, no fears, this lad's fate is not for me
It's the love of people who care that sets me free
But for this son, his time among us is at an end
Liberate your soul dear boy, goodbye my unknown friend

David Cairns HMP Exeter

I'll Wait For You My Darling

I'll wait for you my darling
Till the sun no longer shines
And everybody on this earth
Know that's a long, long time
I'll wait for you my sweetheart
Till the rivers all run dry
Because your love is worth it
I'll wait until I die
I'll wait for you my loved one
There is no one else for me
I don't care if its forever
Is that's the way it has to be
I'll wait for you my darling
Because you showed me love so true
There is no one else I'd ever want
My love is waiting here for you

Danny Carney HMP Everthorpe

My fella bought them in a sale
His taste is ok mostly
It's maybe just that to a male
Green doesn't seem so ghostly

I didn't want to make him weep
I know he meant it well
But while I'm here I'll always keep
Them hidden in my cell

So when I cannot tell you why
My smalls are never seen
Don't think of me as rude or shy
Just picture me in green

Anne Carroll (Prison supplied)

Staying Out

Will you bang me up tonight, Guv'nor dear?
Lock me in snug an' tight (Dull and drear)
I just thought you ought a know
That it's time for me to do
An' they'll never ever get me back in 'ere

Am I happy here in jail, Buddy dear?
Makes me want to weep and wail! (Shed a tear)
An empty cell they'll find
'Cos I'm leaving you behind
An' they'll never ever get me back in 'ere

Does the meth go down a treat, Nursey dear?
When you got the H well beat (No more gear)
Now I don't get off me face
I'll rejoin the human race
An' they'll never ever get me back in 'ere

Is the old clock standing tall, Mother dear?
In a corner of the hall (Year on year)
For such domestic bliss
I am leavin' all of this
An' they'll never ever get me back in 'ere

Does the long grass wave and sway, Father dear?
Round the hidden winding way (Coast is clear)
To a secret shady nook
Where the boys in blue won't look
So they'll never ever get me back in 'ere

Mel Carter HMP Littlehey

48

All The Clothes On The Pipes!

All of the clothes on the pipes outside each cell
Represent a different life inside of this hell
One T-shirt, two T-shirt, three T-shirt, four
Each has its own life dripping water to the floor

All of the clothes on the pipes outside each cell
Show a different personality or soul I can tell
Adidas, Armani or G-Star Raw
Each label a blood group or prison number on the door

Some like the greys of the prison issue
With the drab boring colour of the junkies grey hue
Then there's the Armani of the dealer next door
Dressed to the nines with this money from the score
Full of shit and hate for the man he helped to floor
Full of discontent nothing more that's for sure

All of the clothes on the pipes outside each cell
Tells me a story of one's life in a shell
The Adidas of the hoodie the street thug on a fool
The wannabe gangster the kid and street mule

All of the clothes on the pipes outside each cell
Reminds me of a tale of how each of us must have fell
All colours of the rainbow like leaves on a tree
Which shine like a beacon of the season his sentence came to be

Then there's the clothes on the pipes outside my cell
Washed in my sink with my hands they miss that smell
Of the summer blooms the winters fuel
The laffs of the kids or hey left the house for the school
The missus's smell the love on all the smiles on her face
See my clothes are my blanket that can remove me from this place

My clothes on the pipes outside of my cell
See they remind me of my life and the soul I used to sell
I was no different from the rest as I've got the lot
Coz I've been every person nothing more I've not forgot

See the clothes on the pipes outside of my cell
Remind me of mad times on some tales I'm afraid to tell
They show me the errors of this life I've come to lead
And remind me of the smells and the women that I need
I will wear them with pride till we're together and I'm freed
As it's your memories that I cherish and your words that I heed

Matty Cartwright HMP Stoke Heath

Jangling Keys

Jangling keys
And sugarless teas
Plastic knives and forks

The banging doors
And mopping floors
Around the yard we walk

Cell inspection
Self reflection
The Chaplin wants to talk

The applications
And associations
Locks, bells, and bars

Education
And visitations
Parole and E.D.Rs

The pat downs and searches
The multi faith churches
And the odd game of cards

Medication
And meditation
The detox is really hard

The clenched up fists
For your canteen lists
Should have never got in debt

You did your crime
Now do your time
There's no need to fret

Now your time is done
It's time to get out
But if you think it's over
You've learned bleeding nowt

Justin Catlow HMP Nottingham

Prison Life

The darkest nights
Through the longest days
Regretting my mistakes
Heading myself astray

Hurting inside
Building up pain
Losing everything
With nothing to gain

First time locked up
It's not what it seems
Cheap sh***y razors
No shaving cream

Cuts on the surface
Deeper inside
Man gets wrapped up
Loses his pride

Prison life is different
Enough time to think
Talking about their crimes
Some on the brink

The edge of insanity
People here for life
Some with kids
And even a wife

Second chances are golden
Few men get this
You should treasure them carefully
Just like that very first kiss

I wish I was free
Not locked up in here
To live my life
Without any fear

A promise I'll make
To myself and to you
To make everything better
For my daughter Amelia
I LOVE YOU

Lee Chapman HMP Chelmsford

Subbies: Coming Up For Air

Subbies, suboxene, subversive, sub-lingual
Its substitute prescribing in medical circles
Safer than methadone, so I'm told
But so hard to kick when they get a hold

They come blistered and bound
Like I am now
Little pills, no cheap thrills
But trouble will follow and how

I'd stutter, stumble and have the aches
Without my supply of twos and eights
I should've have known better but I'm not that clever
Now banged up, not banging up, for what seems like forever

Cluckin' at Christmas and a turkey
Druggins a horrid underworld and so murky
I'm lucky the health team here's so good
Or I might have harmed myself if I could

I've been red-carded and sent off the pitch
Rightly so 'cos I'm not match fit
My life will change with this stretch
When I come out I wanna be my best

So I'm cleaning up for the New Year
No more drugs or booze or cigarettes
I'm in the sin-bin that's fair enough
Though I can't honestly say I've no regrets

Pain killers: ironic how they can cause so much pain
And for this addict I need to re-wire my brain
The devil got in me that's for sure
But I won't let that happen anymore

Tough talk has been good for me
I know ill recover, gradually
I made a bad decision and I will pay the price
And on reflection this prison may have saved my life

Gordon Chorlton HMP Guernsey

What I See Is Green

The city lights cause such awe
Reflect in puddles on the floor
Do I stop or go? Do I stop or go?
Confusing worries that I can't slow
You fetched a rainbow from where you'd been
Everything's red, but what I see is green

Through highs and lows of chemical moods
The fads and trends and vegan foods
Are we normal yet? Are we normal yet?
I just knew I'd win our formal bet
A rush of adrenaline and you lost your spleen
Everything's red, but what I see is green

You woke and you changed and you launched into space
Screamed as my gravity pulls down your face
Our love was so real, our love was so good
Can't forget about you while I'm covered in blood
Your heart bled to grey so as not to be seen
Everything's red, but what I see is green

I wished and I hoped and I prayed and I raged
I e-mailed and texted, I phoned and I paged
Can you hate me now? Can you hear me now?
Reciprocate - to show me how!
Look what you've done; done to my dreams
Everything's red, but what I see is green

The station lights that buzz with my pain
Of nervous hues refracting through rain
Your time has come, your time has come
Say the railway lines that whisper and hum
Level crossings of life and death are obscene
Everything's red, but what I see is green

Tom Clark HMP Wakefield

White Scabs

Those crispy, crunchy, blobs of toothpaste
Clinging to the walls
Where pictures were once mounted
They live in groups of fours
Where many men have hung their pics
Of woman in the raw
The white scabs are all they leave
As they walk out the door

Gareth Clark HMP Lewes

So I'm Stuck In La Moye

So I'm stuck in La Moye, for being a bad boy
Cops on my tail, no chance of bail
This is my story I'd like to unveil
You can't beat the system am I destined to fail?
For the chance of my freedom I will fight tooth and nail
So I'm adjusting to jail
Been receiving some mail
Hearing from loved ones
Puts wind in my sail
I'm on remand you see, forever waiting
For the judge to hear my plea
How I miss my beautiful children
This wasn't mean to be, please God
Watch over them until they set me free
So I'm doing my chores mopping the floors
Can't get my head round the 'slamming of doors'
Or the 'jangle of keys'
Guess it could be worse, could have head lice or fleas!
So I'm becoming a menace at table tennis
Ping pong on the wing out on a sting
I'll pay you for the chocolate or a Haribo fizzy thing
But then again I would trade them in
To hear a sweet sound of a song bird sing
But I'm stuck in La Moye

Neil Martin Coleman HMP La Moye

Regret

Looking back life was so happy, a good job
Five great kids, and a wife, still looking so pretty

Christmas coming, a real time of joy, to see the smiling facing of grandkids
When they say open their toys

I want to give them all, everything that they deserve
That's who I am, so extra money required and to plan a safe scam!

This opportunity will never come again, enough for comfort
Especially at my age, so simple a job, so much to gain!

So here I sit writing these words of woe, locked up in prison
Trapped, with nowhere to go

Christmas still to come, no job, no money, a wife
Full of tears, bills to pay, food to buy, she's living in fear

No smiles on grandkids faces, all dreams washed away
Unable to hold them, just here locked away

'Why' what makes us do this? When all was so well
Such stupid mistakes of greed, that leaves you in hell

Now, so much regret, the pain I have caused, sadness and sorrow
Forget the plan and the scam, they and I hate the man I am!

P Coombes HMP Belmarsh

Seven

I first saw you laughing
And all I could do was smile
It began:
Star-crossed lovers

We explored the seven sins together

Lust,
We forgot we needed to breathe

Pride,
Who would say 'I love you' first

Glutton,
We know it's bad for us

Greed,
Demanding each other's attention

Envy,
When jealousy reared its ugly head

Anger,
When we fought

Sloth,
Becoming too comfortable to show we cared

You held me tight
And I wouldn't let go
I didn't want you too
I didn't want to say goodbye

Forever friends
But I can't pretend
I still love you

Craig HMYOI Polmont

Strings

She stood and looked towards me, then caressed my hand
Surprised; with solid belief, at how she took command
And without a word stared into my soul
And in my life soon stole the starring role

She skipped the script and declared 'I love you'
And I found myself evolve into anew
And in return, I gave the wordsmith my heart
Haunted by nightmares of being apart

The worst sin is lust, heart full of ache, no trust
A meaningless allure that no one should endure
What you want is not the same as what I need
Look between the lines and take a good read

She whispered sweet nothings and that's what they are
Leaving me with nothing but an emotional scar
It's all an illusion, with no real conclusion
She's a liar and a cheat, take a ride in a the back seat

She found her way inside my bed
Made her territory inside my head
A user and an abuser, it's all her, her, her
Don't let her win, don't fall to the sin

She poisoned me quickly without warning
Symptoms of the seven sins; I'm possessed
I devolve more each and every morning
Controlled by own lust and greed, I'm obsessed

She became my master and I her puppet
With strings attached became her Muppet

Craig HMYOI Polmont

Get An App

There's an app for that
There's an app for this
There's soon to be an app
To take a piss

Fill in your name
Fill in your number
Get it into the box
Before you slumber

Wait some days to get a reply
Look up in the sky for pigs to fly
If it comes, it won't fill your need
It's not that often those apps succeed

There's only one way to be
Sure it will work
To plead for something
Without feeling a jerk

It's simple, it's easy, it's no great task
Put your app in the bin
And don't bother to ask!

S Croucher HMP Leicester

My Prison Cell

Whitewashed walls, heavy blue door
Filthy lino on the floor
A window that hardly shows the days
The smoke from a roll up creates a haze
This is my home now, though it feels like hell
A room with a bed, a prison cell

A bowl of porridge, a slice of bread
Terrible thoughts that swirl in my head
The sound of silence, the uniform of grey
The feelings of loneliness that fill a long day
This is my home now, though it feels like hell
A room with a bed, a prison cell

No one to share my laughter
No one to see my tears
No one to reassure me and melt away my fears
This is my home now, though it feels like hell
A room with a bed, a prison cell

It's not for pity that I write this rhyme
I've done the crime and I'll do the time
But let those who read this know, it's not a breeze
To be a prisoner doesn't come with ease
This is my home now, my living hell
A room with no heart, my prison cell

S Croucher HMP Leicester

All The Fun Of The Fair-Ly Ancient

This duffer's roller coaster existence
Has hit the buffers of early old age
Like a waltzer that's spun quite some distance
How many revs I've got left's hard to gauge
All my merry-go-rounds are slowing down
As youth's helter-skelter urges expire
With funfair flair I once lit up the town
Now all heat's gone from that burning desire
It's replaced by chilling thrills of a chase
Where the Grim Reaper races after me
Through halls of mirrors, all wearing the face
Of one more well worn than he used to be
Once in lust, down tunnels of love I'd cruise
Seeking steamy adventures in romance
These days, just to sit and chats what I choose
As my heart gives companionship a chance
Dodgem-like I've been bashed all my career
Yet never completely fallen apart
Hence pride in surviving now outweighs fear
And frees me to be a fun-filled old fart
So, far from bidding life's gun booths goodnight
I'll shoot on in hope of winning a prize
Riding fortune's wheel of woe and delight
I'll thrive on what e'er fate's funfair supplies
Then as the show's closing, let me explain
I won't complain or waste breath asking why
With only love packed, I'll catch God's ghost train
To His heavenly house of fun on high

Brian Darby HMP North Sea Camp

For Jean In January

Winter's sharp teeth bite, its cold venom flows
Through those slow waters it fast turns to ice
Not nice when this first burns then numbs the toes
Freezes tears and nips ears as in a vice
Waspish gale-blown hailstones fair sting my face
Late night and early night dull each bleak day
On slippy paths, I'm all over the place
Amidst frost-bound fog, I'm lost in dismay
Yet such mists make fine lace of cobwebs spun
Glistening snow cloaks drabness with wonder
And though it keeps low, still I glimpse a sun
Whose weakest ray splits my gloom asunder
But while these may my sense of chill subdue
I melt best when thawed by warn thoughts of you

Brian Darby HMP North Sea Camp

Knocked Back

Untie hope's yellow ribbon
And fling it into the flames
Of frustrations paranoia
Turn tear-stung eyes heavenward
To see aspiration's dreams
Go up in procedural smoke
Step back, lest a cataract
Of fast plummeting spirits
Wash away all sense of self-worth
For post deliberation
The Parole Board have spoken
And, in so many words, have said
"No".

Brian Darby HMP North Sea Camp

Front Room

Bif, baf, bop, another clout to the chops
All I wanted was to watch Top of the Pops
Now I'm lying on the floor curled up like a ball
So you can't clout me anymore
But now all you do is kick me like a fucking football
All around our front room
Stop mum, I'm your son
Remember I'm the little one
It's not my fault I was put in your womb
Should have had a condom on
As my dad was a fucking bum
Oh no, now it's his turn to kick me
Round our fucking front room
Up and down the stairs, now I'm black and blue
Look, the police are watching you
Forty six years later I still remember all the beatings
I got from both of you

Dave HMP Blundeston

Family Tree

Me, I'm no criminal hardened
Allowed to work in prison's garden
Great escape from endless bang-ups
With head full of 'unjust' hang ups

I pick up after litter throwers
Or walk behind a little mower
Grow grass grow, a foot a day
So I'm let out to cut the hay

Go on 'bruvver' throw some more
Then I'm not stuck behind the door
With tortured soul therein entombed
In tiny concrete, toilet room

Saw something today upon the grass
Nothing any man had cast
Never noticed before despite its size
Yet was always there before my eyes

It reminded me of all I'd missed
Lost freedom's taste, my children's kiss
Strange here in this land of grey and pink
Where only boy scouts stop and think

How many Prunus cherry-blossom tree
Could so affect a man like me
My granddad's hand, my babies' smiles
All with me now again a while

That cumulonimbus, flowing mass
Like nuclear blast, it held me fast
Mushrooming up to azure blue sky
It made me stop, and stand and cry

Denzil Davies HMP Ranby

Poetry

So the IPP sentence has ended
'Cos 'FOREVER' was never intended
But we still remain
"Arbitrarily detained"
Due to 'RISK' perception, probation pretended!

Denzil Davies HMP Ranby

Prison Library God Send

I read a book by Christopher Hitchens
He called it 'God's Not Great"
All about our different religions
And depths of that debate

Simply put - there is no God
Just nature, the universe and science
Truth be told, it's not so odd
Faiths just reliance - compliance

So I don't believe in God - no more
I've had it - enough's enough
Miracles, heaven? Oh heavens 'NO!'
To bibles and all that stuff

Cats out the bag - 'meow meow'
We're all alone in space
And who to turn to when frightened now?
Just us - the Human Race

Never mind, never mind - we'll be ok
Religion only progress impeded
Killed millions in wars, and still today
Breeds fear and hatred not needed

Hold someone's hand and don't be scared
There's no hell or 'eternal damnation'
Live, love, read books, be prepared -
Only knowledge will bring you salvation

Denzil Davies HMP Ranby

The Bottle Of Britain

My dad used to drink in the officer's club
Battle of Britain refought in the pub
Smiling uncles, cousins whole clan
Downing Jerries and pints - RAF to a man

From generous aunt's glasses 'Now only a sip'
'Don't act 'deft' or you'll get a 'good clip'!
Halcyon days, safe innocent bliss
Association seeded addiction's kiss

Fifteen, drunk, at my sister's wedding
Warning perhaps of where it was heading
Drinking, dancing mates and me like fools
Smoking too, we broke all the rules

Older, no wiser - 'Oh same again'
Hangover daily and 'Never again'
Girlfriends plenty - but first love went
Heartbroken, empty - but I didn't relent

'Settled' at last! Now just 'the odd can'
Wife and kids forged a 'sensible' man
Held a job, drove a Jag, wasn't daft
Drank toasts in the Masons - 'To Queen and Craft'

Made it at last, grandchildren born
All was ok until that shocking morn
I looked at the doc, my wife looked at me
Your throat, he said, it's cancer you see

Shit and Jam, it all went nuts
You can't drink again no ifs or buts
Terror iced me, stared into my grave
Fell to my knees, cried, I couldn't be saved

Rumours of my death prematurely spread
Would my wife soon remarry, once I was dead?
Someone else in my place, my dog at his knee
Our babies calling him granddad instead of me

Oh no, I bottled it, blotted it, drank my way through
Mistakenly thinking it's what real men do
Family and friends all said cut it out
But I bought a Harley once up and about

Continued ...

Eighteen again, there was now no 'tomorrow'
My stupid behaviour caused loved ones such sorrow
Daddy's a drunk, disgrace, check him out!
Alone, despised, all deserved without doubt

So the sum of my fears now become manifest
Kids, home, love - life's work - all gone west
Swept away on a river of Stella
Divorced, wife 'moved on' got a new fella

The Perfect Storm, like dawn had to break
No more, couldn't take, from that nightmare can't wake
My Queen , my castle, my life I claimed back
But drunk, failed, jailed - domestic attack

I survived, I live here inside - dead inside
To all, so sorry I walked the wild side
Oh, sober now, no I don't drink today
Free, but I'm not! And my family pay

Denzil Davies HMP Ranby

Ya Get Me

Easy new brother
You get me
Listen up yeah
Nuff Said

It's all noise shouting out from their heads

Don't make it twisted
Keep the peace Bruv
We're not even related
You know what I mean cous'

Oh the eloquence of prison talk
A Darwinian audition of multicultural acceptance
Of one inmate speaking respect to another
It ain't Gangsta, Rapper or Crow

It's a brother from another
Giving love, peace and respect
A way of finding common ground
In a universally diverse dialect

Ian Day HMP Whatton

I'm Sorry! (Ode To A Wasp)

I sat there eating barbecue chicken, hungry, a little stressed
When someone darted past my face and landed on my chest

I panicked for a microsecond, then quickly blew him off
And picked back up my chicken wrap, I then began to scoff

As tasty as this wrap was to me, it soon became quite clear
That someone else was hungry too and held my chicken dear!

It buzzed back in, now circling, hell bent on that sweet taste
As I tried to blow and sweep away but he persevered with haste!

And then he landed, so arrogant, right on my blue plate!
Impossible, how me so big, for one so small, hold so much hate!

I grabbed my knife, and bent it back, creating kinetic force
I let it go: the wasp got whacked all frantic to the floor!

He lay there weak and barely moved. Broken, deformed, all bent
He made no sound, lay on his back, his short life nearly spent

What agony he must have felt! What pain! What fright! What shock!
If he had been a human being I would have called a doc

Such shame, such guilt my conscience felt. I'm a murderer soon to be
As this poor wasp, lay by himself, dying painfully

I empathised. An idea came; I'd stop this agony
'Sorry' I said, lifted my leg to end his misery

With one big stamp, the poor wasp; crushed, his life all spent, diminished
I glanced and found my chicken wrap, sat on my plate unfinished

My stomach turned, now feeling sick, my wrap had lost its taste
As on the floor, a little splat, poor wasp! Oh, what a waste!

Who was I to take away this life? I never had no right
I got a tissue and picked him up, a truly awful sight!

This tiny wasp, he used to fly; his tiny corpse held life
Until he met this wretched man, his chicken, then his knife

Wrapped in guilt, consumed with sin, I lay him on the ledge
I said 'I'm sorry' and blew him off, into a nearby hedge

That same sweet taste of barbecue, that made my mouth so wet
Became a bitter after taste and brought the poor wasp death!

My chicken wrap had lost appeal. In the bin it would soon go
When suddenly, another wasp, flew through my cell window

I didn't move, I let him be, I let him claim his prize
And anytime now, wasps come near I let them lead their lives!

every time I see a wasp, hornet or bumble bee
I think about my friend the wasp and mumble 'I'm sorry!'

Patrick Diffley HMP Elmley

Counting The Days

As I walk around the yard at night
I close my eyes and see the light
Once I'm obsessed with power and wealth
I'm now filled with love and health
Those first little steps that I never seen
Missed because I was mopping the green
The first song she chose to sing
Missed again, I was cleaning the wing
To see her first day in school, I'd have been so proud
Instead in a gym, busy and loud
Watching her hair growing long and curl
I'm filled with pride "that's my little girl"
They say the best things in life are free
Ask me now, I'd have to agree
The time has come to change if I can
It's time for me to be a man
No need to be depressed and sad
I'm the luckiest man alive, I'm Daisy's dad
As I walk around this yard at night
Counting the days, the future's bright

S Dobson HMP Lowdham Grange

Out Of Sight Out Of Mind

I wasn't surprised to find
Out of sight, out of mind
My so called friends
Aren't there till the end

Cocktails and beers
Nothing was too dear
You were only my friend
When I had the spends

"I'll write you a letter
Or even better
Send me a VO
I'll come and see you Bro"

Well it's out of order
You never used that visiting order
Not even that letter
To make me feel better

Now the cards have been dealt
I can only rely on myself
But I'm not one to moan
Won't be long till I'm home

And the ones that are there
Are my family that care
So they will come first
Not users and flirts

Francis Doherty HMP Thorn Cross

One Night Stand

Afterwards, easing around spines
You fall asleep
That, that funny breath on a tape loop
Odd, I suppose, how noisy silence is
Skin
Mouth
Axe fall clock

The bark of birds that seem to mock

Hey! Were I a lover, friend, even a whore
Not this creature
Not this sand snake signature
On a desert dune
A contour, nothing more

Patrick Donahue HMP Oakwood

No Cure

How can a man who lives in a cell
Learn about heaven while living in hell

How can a man learn to trust those in power
When he's let out his cell for less than an hour

How can a man who's living his fears
Learn about joy while drowning in tears

How can a man learn how to change
When he lives in a world where normal is strange

How can a man mature with age
When most of his life is spent in a cage

How can a man who feels nothing but pain
Hang on to his sanity while going insane

Well if you think the system works
Then your thinking is perverse

For prison cures no one
It always makes you worse

Paul Donlin HMP Wymott

Life Lines

I wait for a letter, you said you wrote
It's been seven long days since we last
Spoke, throw me a life line, some sign of
Hope, I wait for a letter, you told me you wrote

I wait for the letter, you said you did send
If you no longer love me - then why pretend?
You with your freedom - me with no choice
Some words to believe in, a comforting voice

Outside I watch nature, but I'm dying
Inside, still wait for that letter which
Hasn't arrived, you with your dreaming
Here I remain, don't tell me you'll write
Then, stay silent again

It's been too many weeks now since we
Last spoke, and I haven't received the
Letter you wrote. I want to believe
But my spirit is broke as, I wait for
The letter you swore that you wrote

My life is so empty and my heart complains
Crushed by the hollow
False stories you made
Lies and excuses - why don't you explain
Why leave me waiting in hope, again?

If you no longer want me - why still pretend?
Kinder to let this torment end - not fade
Like a promise, between holiday friends
Left waiting in silence, love dies in
The end

Douglas HMP Doncaster

Thoughts

The road is long and strewn with broken glass
And just when I'm thinking I've cracked it
I fall back on my ass
However good things rarely come easy
And never not simply to please me
You reap what you sow
Yeah right even you know
So don't be silly like me and slow
Brush the glass away,
And keep on walking
Time and life is ticking away
No more talking
Tomorrow's not just another day
It's the day you say,
I've had enough of this stuff
Even though I'll be feeling rough
And the daft thoughts of wanting to die
Two weeks down the line instead of craving the high
I'm going to have the fresh air and the sky
And realise silly bollocks here was never going to die
No more
Will I hide from the feeling inside
Yes I'm in a cell
With me the emergency bell
But hey it don't have to be the hell that you once felt
It's all looking rosy and even quite cosy
Don't put things on the back burner
'Cause it's the being straight that's the earner

Gary K Dunn HMP Guys Marsh

Ode To The Wall

Sounds start stirring at 7:30
Medication is dished out through
A small hatch in a narrow corridor
The cogs of the regime are set in motion

The morning bird in amorous flight
Glides by block C, cell six
A welcomed absence from the chill of the night
8ft by 4, a table, a TV, a door

Thick grey concrete decorated
In solid steel barbed wire
Those trees sure seem greener
Flirting with the dancing wind, on the other side

Perched on the clock tower overlooking the green
A bird whistles a song, other birds join in
They're crooning straight at me, vibrations in the breeze
Winter on its knees, places kisses at my feet

Samuel Ellett HMP Norwich

Where I Really Want To Be

A relationship in jail isn't exactly what I planned
Nor is it the perfect place to let our love expand
That's just how it is, although it maybe seems too hard
That doesn't mean we just give up and break each other's heart
Labour of love didn't mean that much before I went to jail
But now I bleed a little bit just waiting for your mail
What do I do? I struggle on 'cause I know it all pans out
'Cause faith in me and faith in you is what it's all about
I think about us every day and count until I'm home
Till then we have our letters and don't forget the phone
Sarah, life has put us both physically apart
But know that all I want to do is live inside your heart

Gareth Evans HMP Grendon

Breaking News

Exclusive! Exclusive! Read all about it!
But if there's no books, how do you go about it?
Go to the library, I'm sure they'll have it
They're cutting the funds, so I seriously doubt it

Exclusive! Exclusive! The prisons are crowded!
Fear not my friend, for that's easily sorted
Expand them! Expand them! That's sure to resolve it
For bigger is better, the problem is sorted!

Exclusive! Exclusive! The wages are falling!
The officer's mess is not just in the kitchen
They're cutting and chopping so workload's increasing
Yet prisons are crowded, the logic's confusing

Exclusive! Exclusive! Make Cat D elusive!
Don't let them go out or they're sure to abuse it
Then when they're released what stops them from
revolting?
Don't hold your breath they get recalled for breathing

Exclusive! Exclusive! The prisons are flooded!
With opiates and sedates and spice has exploded!
Oh how do we combat the nuisance narcotics?
Ban boxers and socks and erm leggings and stockings?

Exclusive! Exclusive! Chris Grayling is growling!
He's huffing and puffing and systems are failing
Now chaos is order, for chaos is Grayling
Surely we see that the end is beginning

Osaheni Evbuomwan HMP Coldingley

I Stay In My Cell

I stay in my cell, the doors are locked
I make origami to pass the time
I made three figures out of paper
I have three sons who I love
I made a shirt out of paper
Outside I would help everyone
I made paper chains so I remember this is a prison
And not to forget I made an elephant
Because my sons say Dad stay strong
I made some camels
They are alone in the desert
They are the ships of the sand
I made some crows I hope they don't eat me
I made some rabbits, they are free and I hope I will be
I still have a family

Seval Fehim HMP Highpoint

My Affair With Miss Brown

She used to visit me day and night, or whenever funds would allow
Especially when me and her indoors would fall out and have a row
And when the old bill wanted me and I had to run and hide
She would never judge me, and always be at my side
I'd wait for her on street corners for hours, it was such a tease
But when she finally did turn up she'd never fail to please
She'd wrap herself around me and put me in a haze
And lock herself away with me, sometimes for days
She'd bed down in my squalor and didn't care if I washed or shaved
And when I was absent she didn't care if I misbehaved
As long as I gave her a call when I found myself ready
She'd come running quick as you like and we'd be going steady
I kept her a secret for so long coz she was so beautiful and royal
But soon I discovered she wasn't being so loyal
I found out she was seeing friends of mine from day to day
And to my surprise they were doing her in a different way
They were seeing her both at work and in their leisure
And that she was giving them less, yet they got more pleasure
We were seeing her three or four times a day, sometimes up to five
It felt like we needed her just to keep us alive
But soon I found out she was stealing pals from their kids and wives
Not happy with doing that she started to take their lives
Twenty two friends and ten years on I've finally had enough
I told Miss Brown to leave and to take all her stuff
It's been a year since she's been absent and now only visits in my dreams
The same deep dark hole where I hear my dead friends screams
And though we have now parted I know that she waits
Offering her open arms when I leave the prison gates
And so during my time I hope to gain the tools to say
No to Miss Brown, I'm keeping her at bay

Fenny HMP Lowdham Grange

Haiku Poetry

Absorbing music
The bars are slowly melting
Going away now

Hot sunny beaches
A hot mince pie and whisky
Back draft memories

Butter flys away
Like milk cheese caterpillars
Feeding animals

Clouds block the sunlight
The fruit machines of nature
Apple paying trees

Sean Fitzy HMP Liverpool

Dementia

She can't remember me being born
She can't remember the chorus at dawn
She can't remember our holidays abroad
She can't remember driving a Ford
She can't even remember my Dad dying
Or me covering up every day and lying
She can't remember getting married
Or the two kids that she carried
She can't remember the good or bad times
Or the days I used to try and write rhymes
The illness has took over her mind
Lost in a world she'll never find
God it hurts me when she cries
Sometimes I wish she would just die
'Cause she's not my mum, not anymore
I lost my mum a long time before
She looks right through me as if I'm not there
With a blank expression and a long dreamy stare
Pale faced with fleck of grey in her hair
Where is my mum coz her mind isn't there
Lord why do this to her, it's just not fair
I'm so sorry mum that I can't be there
But please don't think that I just don't care
I do, I love you, and soon I'll be there

Trevor Flay HMP Moorland

Finding The Courage

Black eye
And heart again broken
Each new bruise worn
Like some kind of sick token
Busted lip
Another bloody nose
When the next attack will be
She doesn't know
She's tried leaving
Once or twice before
But there he always was
Between her and the door
Not really understanding
Why she loves him still
Seems so long ago now
Since he broke her will
Curled up crying
Feeling more and more alone
When did this house
Stop feeling like a home?
Trapped in this prison
That she longs to escape
Desperate to be rescued
Before it's too late
Another beating
More blood and tears
She's lost so much of herself
Throughout the years
Suicide attempt
The summer before last
'Attention seeking' he'd called it
She's getting nowhere fast
Laughing mockery
As he knocks her to the floor
Trying to protect herself
She can't take much more
Somehow though
She finds the inner strength
To keep on fighting -
She takes a deep breath
Now at last
She's found the courage to leave
Walking to freedom
Away from the beast
No more his prisoner

Continued ...

The bonds she had to break
With this new found independence
A better life awaits
Bruises fade
Mental scars take longer
But she's her own person again
And already feeling stronger

Lee Fox HMP Lincoln

It Never Fails

I wanted to believe in you
In what you say
And do
I wanted to believe

I wanted to drink your dogma
Until I was intoxicated
Then sublimated
By you

I wanted to follow your path
'til I heard you laugh
At God
And His angels

I wanted to hold your hand
Through the desert
To the promised land
Of our dreams

Damn... I don't think you
Know what I mean

I just wanted to love you
Like a secret sauce
And Holy Communion
But, that's all ruined

Maybe love never fails
But I'm an infidel

Brian Franklin
Thames Calipatria State Prison

I Am

I am Beethoven without pen paper string or piano
A man that's extremely gifted but no tools to express my talents
I am two warring tribes
Two opposing sides
Of one troubled mind
That's divided by the distance you find between the two ends of the spectrum
I am Sun Tzu military strategic fighting internal misconceptions
I am without question the personified essence of imperfect perfection
Hindered only by my own pessimistic mental projections
And that's why I am not a king yet
I am the architect of my own cat A prison
That keeps me bound confined and trapped within this position
Where I am unable the grasp for to reach my goals and ambitions
And if at first this verse seems negative then close and you'll see it's encoded with optimism
Because if you read between the lines you will find
I am the voice that you find deep within side you
That whispers the secret to your soul
That you are the only person stopping yourself from achieving anything that you put your mind to

Vaughan Gannon HMP Forest Bank

First Impressions

He gives me a fist punch
And calls me his brother
He's got me confused
Or he's mixed up with some other

But that's how they talk
This kids using slang
Acting all big in this prison
In front of his gang

I walk off rubbing past him
And up to my pad
En suite loo, and a bunk bed
A TV, not bad

This kid's at my door
He's like "What's up my brother"
Oi you don't know me
Or even my mother...

So what with your lingo
Calling me brother

How can I help you
Or what can I do
Trying to act big
With your bit so solid crew

Calm down, calm down
Take it easy my brother
I've just come to ask
For a lend of some sugar

Lee Goldsworthy HMP Durham

Girlfriends

The woman of the past keep phoning
There was another yesterday arrived from out of state
She wanted to see me
I told her 'no'
I don't want to see them, I won't see them
It would be awkward, gruesome and useless
I know some people who can watch the same movie more than once
Not me
Once I know the plot, once I know the ending
Whether it's happy or unhappy or just plain dumb
Then for me that movie is finished forever
And that's why I refuse to let any of my old movies
Play over and over again for years

Richard Goss HMP Stocken

Love And Kisses (For Natalie)

Love and kisses
From me to you
Love and kisses
For our kids too
Love is a description
Kisses for affection
All the joys of the world
A feeling indescribable
Pure affection inside
One look at my babies
Brings butterflies inside
A kiss so passionate
It lights up the eyes
More beauty than a rainbow
Up in the sky
Love and kisses
For you from me
One second lasts forever
Whilst I'm at your side
One second away
Seems a life time
So this is to you
To devote my love
Forever and always
  XoxoX

Richard Green HMP Northumberland

First Time In

Well, well, well, it's my first time inside
Bars on the windows and nowhere to hide
Anxiety kicks in, stress building high
Eyes are damp and mouth is dry
Inmates they stare as you come through the door
Head stays down and eyes trace the floor
Ceilings are high, windows are small, I'm not even six foot tall
Looking at screws, craning my neck
A muffty off them I'd probably hit the deck
Things in here will never be fine, can't afford to step out of line
I weigh up the odds to see what's for me
Find something in common that might just help me
There's no creature comforts, no sofa no bath
No gadgets or gizmos, just inmates and staff
All that I've got is this military regime
That's no sort of life for any lad it seems
I pick myself up and brush myself down
Start a new day with a smile not a frown
Mix with the lads and try fitting in
Soon I'll be out of here with a fucking big grin

Tony Gunn HMP Haverigg

A Shock From The System

Sideways glances on echoing landings
Whispers and rumours and misunderstandings
Another new cell mate, crimes seldom mentioned
Festering grudges and simmering tensions
Queuing for food that's barely worth eating
Cursing the cold and berating the heating
The fetid reek of ennui lingers
On sallow complexions and nicotine stained fingers
Tattoos tell the tale of past life connections
To sad small town gangs and the need for attention certain that the guy
In cell 305, hates you even though you've no idea why
Some people in here don't het the concept of waiting
They push to the front and blatantly push in
Inside you bridle, seethe and protest
Outside you stay calm, or try your best
To hide the impotent anger and rage
Coz it's best to stay silent, don't confront or engage
In pointless battles you know you can't win
You swallow your pride, develop think skin
A day an revolve on such simple things
A letter from friends and the news that they bring
But it's gone 4pm, hope turns to dread
Hey Guv, any mail? ...a shake of the head
So you sit on your bed riding tides of emotion
That trickle of doubt forms a river, an ocean
Perhaps on the outside they no longer care
Have they found someone else? ...too much to bear
So you swop your last burn and your evening meal
For an illicit pill to assuage the pain that you feel
And so each day passes, doors open, they close
Time loses its meaning and goodness knows
The frightening thing
Is how quickly you find yourself accepting, adapting.

Nick Haines HMP Winchester

Who And Where Am I?

How many years to go, will I ever know
Who or where am I?
Carved your name upon my heart
No longer entwined, we lie apart

I feel we're drowning, not heaven sent
My spirit broken, yours for rent
No more future of love and hope
Gave you a rose, you gave me a rope

Served my head upon a plate
The only comfort for you to take
You say I'm jealous, I'm unkind
I never chose to leave you behind

I see times are dark to come
Too much passion come undone
A bitter pill for me to take
I the ruined fraud and fake

Now all alone I'll bide my time
Nothing left for me that's mine
No something borrowed, something blue
Now just me .... no longer you!

Jim Hainey HMP Kirkham

'Mum' Is Just A Word To Some

Mum is just a word to some
But to me it's so much more
You're the one who taught me to spread my wings
You gave me the courage to soar
High above the life I lived
To leave it all behind
You never lost your faith in me
It wasn't hard for you to find
The memory of your little girl
With pigtails in her hair
That ambitious little madam
Wish not a single care
She made mistakes along the way
But you always helped her to see
The potential in her life
The woman she could be
But time and time again
She'd disappoint you with her choice
Until finally, she listened to your voice
"I'll always love you, no matter what"
Is what you said to me
And now I'm locked inside this cell
But finally I'm free
Free of all the wrongs I chose
Free of all the pain
But now I truly understand
That inside you feel the same
So many nights you stayed up late
That fear inside so raw
In case that doorbell ever rang
And a copper stood at your door
You once told me how you'd waited
To hear that I was dead
Terrified for your little girl
The tears you must have shed
I never stopped to think
What I was doing to you and dad
I always just assumed
If I came home you would be mad
How selfish I was to act that way
And still not understand
But now these walls have cleared my mind
And how I log to hold your hand
Just like when I was a little girl
With pigtails in my hair

Continued ...

Finally I see the pain I caused
And that I cannot bare
You've always been the perfect mum
Trying to guide me along my way
And even though I'm crying now
I can hold my head up high and say
That you didn't fail me mum
I only have myself to blame
I'm so proud and lucky to have you in my life
I just beg you feel the same
You see mum is a word to some
To me it's so much more
You are the strength I aspire to be
You've opened up the door
I'll come home to you soon and show you
I swear you'll be amazed
For now I am becoming
The Angel that you raised

Victoria Hall HMP Downview

Portland Lad

I long to feel your touch
Your fingers on my skin
Your soft lips pressed on mine
And the butterflies within
I yearn to feel your breath
Linger on my neck
And send that shiver through me
Kissing, just a gentle peck
The kind of pecks that tease me
How I wish for you to please me
This feeling just won't leave me
I'm such a worked up mess
I can't help but dream about you
Spend all bang up thinking of you
Countless scenarios on replay
Mind in overload each day
December won't come quick enough
That visit won't be long enough
And once over I'll return
And replay them once again

Victoria Hall HMP Downview

I Know Sorry Doesn't Fix It

Forgive me for the times when I know not quite what to write
Sometimes it seems, then drunk and scared, my instinct is to fight
I feel so helpless stumbling; my whole life is upside down
An absent cure, a time machine, would flip things back around
I'd go back to the night I hurt you, stop. Walk out the door
Before the situation escalated, leaving blood dripping on the floor
Needless to say, it was ME, who was wrong, regardless of your part
I had no right to wound you, scarring your face and both our hearts
To reconcile, hear me apologise, might aid you to recuperate
I yearn forgiveness from you, but now I, you must hate
I never intended to hurt you, or be so drunk I lost control
Your life has been affected and mine now, and endless hole
Of guilt, regret, hysteria, each and every waking day
You did not ask nor deserve it, so prison is the price I pay
A million ways I've played it back, a million times I've cried
From my crime I cannot run because there's nowhere left to hide
Please, I beg you don't hate me, for that night I was not ME
I know sorry doesn't fix it, so I wish that you could see
The knock on effect to both our lives and our families
I did not know I was capable, of such a violent crime
Intended or not, it was my choice, to avoid drawing the line
But I do not have a time machine, just a vivid memory
The most powerful thing, neither can escape, so I can never be free
You must absolutely despise me I would not blame you if you do
To avoid alcohol and confrontation is something I now choose
PLEASE believe me when I say I'M SORRY, for causing you such pain
That night I was just an angry drunken mess, there was nothing positive I gained
So here it is, my thoughts and fears, in a poem to make me feel better
Because when trying to write to you directly, I struggle with a letter

Rebecca Halliday HMP Eastwood Park

Victim's Family

I apologise for what I did, I know you must be hurting
The anger in your heart really must be burning
I understand every night why you're tossing and turning
That sick feeling in your stomach must feel like its churning
I can't apologise enough for what I have done
At the time it seemed like it was fun
I was a kid with no money and also on the run
No excuse please don't feel like I've won
If I could change what I did I would have
I would have chosen to go down the good path
Like I should have
Instead of the mugs path
I know you probably hate me because I'd feel the same
I've caused you nothing but grief and a lifetime of pain
That's why I'm here trying to make a change
Writing this feels a little bit strange
Tell your family I'm also sorry for the pain I've caused
Taking belongingss that were not mine but yours

Jordan Hart Youth Offending Staffordshire

Ode To Veronica

Oh Veronica
I remember the day we met
It was hot, steamy and wet
Who'd have thought that in less than an hour
You'd be coming back to my place from the L-wing shower
It wasn't an easy relationship
I resented your presence
Lurking
Always there like a reminder not to tread dangerously
Oh but we've shared some time together Veronica
When I finally got a cell to myself
You were there
When my flip-flops were confiscated due to an admin cock-up
You were there
When apps went unanswered and V.Os went AWOL
You were a healing comfort
I'm sure you've felt unwanted and unloved
Yet you stuck with me
For two sodding years
Despite the Wartner, Cuplex and Salactol
And pumice stone that took an age to arrive
But now Veronica
Our relationship has run its natural course
There's a big freeze coming so I hear
You'll be in safe hands
Or feet if you prefer
For myself
And on behalf of my whole body
I'm sending you off to the world of Chiropody
Where you're no doubt considered a bit of a looker
With that seductive black spot and hard skin
Who couldn't resist?
But looker or no looker
It's time I said goodbye to my prison verruca
Farewell oh flakey one
Oh great wartness

Robin Hart HMP La Moye

Prison Life

Prison life these days is so sick
I pull out my remote and turn channels with a flick

When bored of my TV I'll put on my blaster
Then PS2 time to make time go faster

Electric and heating on 24/7 night and day
For the TV license is a pound a week we pay

Everything is free, food, butlers and chefs
Every day we get this, fuck this is the best

Chill out on the wing, then chill out at work
Then go to our visits eating munch like dessert

Come back for phone call and shower
Chill with the lads playing pool for an hour

This is luxury, this is great
Freedom comes one day and out through the gates
It's time to go now, I'll see you all soon
When I come back in with me bed pack, knife fork and spoon!

Chris Hartley HMP Wealstun

Silent As Winter

My entire life has been filled with silence
Nothing to be said about the rules in my life
I couldn't bear people to know how bad, disgusting, horrible I was
Silent as winter

RULE 1: close your eyes
So as not to see anything
RULE 2: cover your ears
So as not to hear anything
RULE 3: shut your mouth
So as not to say anything
Silent as winter

And just the same as winter comes
The silence comes too
The snow falls and lies on the ground
You look back at the tracks left in the snow
The same as you look back at your life
You see the marks left in the snow
By the hurt, the fear and the silence

It's a silence you hear when you sit among the graves
The birds in the sky
The wind through the trees
And the distant sound of children playing

You picture them running about
Playing games, having fun
You see her, in her dress
Her shoes, her hair
Then you recognise - it's you
Running about having fun
But having no one to share her secret with
So, staying silent as winter

You grow up and the fear grows with you
The fear of it carrying on
The fear of someone finding out
Would you be rejected for what you did or did not do

You don't know the answers
So you just carry on
Fearing the worst, hurting inside, being alone
But most of all
Being silent as winter when it comes

Heidi Hope Scott Clinic

The Two Chris's

I was all alone
Rotting in my cell
Then in walked Chris
Clean and strong as hell

I was quite happy
Doing my own thing
Then Chris said
Fuck this, let's clean everything!

He'd done 10 years
Some Cat A
And was determined
To get his own way

He didn't boast
Just mentioned some of his old mates
Like John Pilli
Who'd done 41 years without a penny

It started with a cell clean
Then it was me
Shower, shave, haircut, laundry, training!
And now the other Chris is ME

Chris Hill HMP Birmingham

Keeping In Touch

What did we do before there were mobile phones?
And cars that could drive us to and from home?
Buses and trains that could take us places
Internet, Facebook with everyone's faces
One click of a button and the world's at your call
Someone always there whenever you fall
Two or three minutes and you receive a text back
Hardly any time spent, pen and paper sacked
Need information sent, just send a fax
All this technology, so easy to do
Ringing, clicking, surfing its true...
To forget what it's like to be all alone
To wait for contact from anyone at home
To be lost and lonely was once something we forgot
Because talking through science was easy as tying knots
Don't ever take for granted your family and friends
Because when you're in prison, it all comes to an end
Time becomes your enemy and letters take a while
And words become harder like walking green mile
Emotions run wild and frustration takes over
You suddenly wish you could find a four leaf clover
So what was it like before we had mobile phones?
Don't come to prison and you will never know

Ruth Hillman HMP Bronzefield

Speaking Out!

From pillar to post, from door to door
Observing the rich, living with the poor

Success never felt it
Nor have the intellectual capacity to comprehend it
Wish it was a commodity, so I could buy it or lend it

Guns and roses, concrete jungle a confused bundle
Not one direction
More like equilibrium

Born in a family, trapped in society
No sign of Allah
No sign of piety

The only role models for inner city
Hoodlums are rapping about guns, drugs, women and
making millions
It's confusing as hell, and those who feels it knows it
Studying it from a book is nowhere near the same
Yet they point their fingers and dictate the blame

You don't even know me
Never even met me
One mistake and I'm the public enemy

Befriend the strong to control the poor
Supply the rebels with guns, it's not even your war
Poverty and affluence
Violence and war
Seems to be the focus more and more
The rich get richer, the poor stay poor
Fear and greed builds more and more

They say that slavery is over and they kicked out racism
Sentencing guidelines
Analysing statistics!
Corrupting authorities
Infiltrating ballistics
20 years on, the Lawrence's still don't get justice
Drug dealers go to jail
Child abusers are let out on bail
The facts are visible
It's no fairytale

Continued ...

Greed and fear, rich and poor
Love and hate
All of this causes us to separate
Feeling desperate? T's a matter of time
Before you bite the bait

Failing systems, public sector, the cracks are appearing
The ceiling is leaking
Redundancies and negligence now transparent to all
The economies on a rise
Not before we fall

Unsustainable wages, unsustainable jobs
Billions in taxes where's it all gone
55% of youth unemployed, degrees with honours, masters
PHDs and youthful age
Still no jobs, not even at minimum wage

Still we have money to assist other countries in war
Addicted to power, greed, want, more and more

Ryan Horner HMP Northumberland

Stella And Vindaloo

I once met a woman, her name was Vindaloo
He home was Mumbai, India, nowhere near Peru

Her cousin was from Belgium using the name of Stella
She moved herself to England, 'cos of a nasty fella

Vindaloo came to England, as Stella was upset
She resided with her cousin, in her cosy maisonette

To cheer Stella up, rid her of her frown
She took her cousin out for a night on the town

Vindaloo was hot, driving the men wild
Her fiery temper meant, she was anything but mild

Stella was in contrast, simply quite refreshing
Bubbly and cool keeping the men guessing

Approached by a man, using the name of Conrad
Vindaloo's reply was spicy, whist Stella's wasn't too bad

After they had left the club, they returned to Stella's place
Conrad made himself comfy, in front of the fireplace

He kissed Vindaloo, trying to quench his desire
Radiating heat from her lips, she left his mouth on fire

Needing to douse the flames, and put the fire out
"Stella get me water" he began to shout

After bringing water, Stella kissed him too
Suddenly the air was cool, at this bijou rendezvous

He woke the next day, his head really sore
Peering in the mirror, gawped at what he saw

There was a loud rumble, he looked down at his belly
Dashing to the loo, his legs went like jelly

Sitting in reflection, knowing what to do
He made himself a promise. No more Stella and Vindaloo

Nigel Hunter HMP Manchester

Breaking Out

Automatic pilot enveloped in grey
Black crows beckon on the wakening day
Feathers buffeted against the silky grain
Streamline smoothness torn by gust and flurry and rain
I - ain't in no mood nor hurry, gentle breeze in my room
Doesn't fully portray the storm in my gloom
I - tired of waking
I - tired of sleeping
I - tired of walking
I - tired of squawking
I - need to lie down
I - need to get up
My only comfort coffee in my cup
Cannot smell, cannot tell
Cannot question this living hell
I - a tortoise living in my shell
A shell of the man I used to be
A fine figure of a man
And now, like life, emerging
Like the first glimpse of bird or tortoise's beak
From inside a shell, tapping away
From the inside out, a world full of doubt
Will I spread my wings and fly
Will I curl up, crumple, whither, and die?

Michael Irwin HMP Magilligan

Mandisa: The Hidden Side

I lay my envious gaze upon her
She is so beautiful, so lovely
Her smile so radiant
Her laugh too cheerful
She is the light to my darkness, and her happiness outshines my anger
I am weak, but she has the strength of a god
She can care without a doubt, whereas I do not care at all
Her love is endless but my love is non-existent
I have endured so much pain, whilst her heart has never seen hurt
I am lost and have lost myself along the way, but she has never strayed
She stayed pure, angel white
My world turned dark, innocence stripped

Mandisa and I were once so close
From our bond which seemed inseparable, I was forced to walk away
Though we went our separate ways, I do hope we meet again
How long will it take to find my way?
Not many oceans I hope
Alas, my breathing is becoming haggard and my body withering away

You see Mandisa completes me, my life quickly ending without her
I need her to survive, I need her within me
For I am Mandisa, and Mandisa is me

Gholda James HMP Bronzefield

Just Me

Raised by the Government
A product of the system
Never known a family
So I've never really missed them
Never get a visit
Never get a letter
Never tried to fool myself
That it will get better
Haven't got a girlfriend
Haven't any children
Haven't any hopes and dreams
So I'll never fulfil them
I don't have a future
And I have no past
Not a single soul will miss me
When I breathe my last
Just me against the world
Just me, myself and I
Sometimes I force aloud a laugh
But inside I slowly die
I hear people whinge
Because their visit might be late
Or they had no ID
And got stopped at the gate
Be grateful you fools
Be glad that they are there
Be happy you know not my lonely despair
I have no friends
I have no family
I have no one to write to
And no one comes to visit me
So count your blessings
And count your lucky stars
While I count my days as these
Lonely years pass

Jason HMP Stocken

Village Life

Some people lose their hearts to city life
But the village I am from is so much more beautiful
There is something magical you can only find in the village
That you cannot find in any city

In the village there is beauty
In the village there are rivers, streams and spectacular sunsets to see
In the village drums beat, cymbals chime, bangles tinkle, anklets jangle and ears ring
In the village everyday is a festival
In the village are my people, my ties
In the village there is a simplicity, modesty and shyness
In the village there is happiness, peoples' hearts are golden

One day soon I'll be away from this pollution and these fast cars
One day soon I'll be away from the noisy clubs, pubs and bars
I swear all of this noise is making me feel ill
One day soon I'll be going back home, where I can be still

Shahzad Javed HMP Low Moss

A Lifetime Of Dreams

To be a princess
Magic powers, fairy dust
My dreams as a child
These were a must

Then I get older

To be a nurse
A dancer, to teach
As a teenager
These were in my reach

Then I got older

I changed my mind
Mistakes were made
My original dreams
Started to fade

Now I am older

My dream is to be free
To be settled with my family
That all I want as a mum
My son, my daughter and me

Jennifer HMP Askham Grange

Road To Recovery

My heart enslaved death engraved
Addiction plus affliction equals rage
But to accept the things I cannot change
Dissipates the chains from my cage

Pain built the walls of this dam
It fed the disease, the addict I am
But to have courage to change the things I can
Is the true making of a man

So I stand in the faithful circle of sobriety
Cocooned by humility humble by humanity
God grant me the serenity
Each day to conquer this insanity

Jim E HMP Swaleside

All That Glitters

She takes me everywhere with her
I've seen so many places
I'm almost as close to her as her own skin
I realise I am not the most valuable
Or glamorous that she has
But I'm special and sentimental
When she feels low
I am here to give her a feeling of assurance
I am tarnished, out of shape, I've lost my sparkle
But she loves me as much today
As the day she first set her eyes upon me
My colourful beauty and perfect clarity has faded
Through the years, but I'm with her at all times
Apart from when she takes time away to bathe or shower
She will twist me with care and place me not too far away from her
I always get back to my warm home
When she gently places me back where I belong
The things I've heard and places I have seen
Like a fly on the wall
I came from far away and have travelled everywhere
Closely with her ever since
I don't need to speak to reassure her
When she feels weak, she just gazes at me
I was given to her as a symbol of commitment
I hold the hope that everything will be ok
I being back her memories the happy and the sad
I am solid and dependable
I am a memory of the person who gave me to her
I will always be loved, I'm that special ring

Jodie A HMP Askham Grange

Lost

Circumnavigating between the air vents
In search of my inner essence
My spirits lost I'm in a strange place
Pure confusion upon my face
Can a leopard change it spots?
Inner essence I miss you lots
This strange place is a bit familiar
Authority's voice sounds so similar
You're a heartless thug get your arse in line
This is the baggage that comes with my crime
This is the method to finally beat me
I can't help feeling they're trying to cheat me
Misunderstood with my northern accent
All my conditions are pure entrapment
Prison or police it's all the same
How do I forget this negative fame?
The day has come to get my shoes on
I have no clue where to move on
Which borough do I make my mark?
Or is it a tent in some park?

Daniel Joslin HMP Highdown

My Bald Hairless Head

The ministry of justice don't know the score
Who in their right mind gives Jimmy Saville
The keys to Broadmoor
Don't even think I'm gonna stop there
Let me tell you about the stresses that have contributed
To losing my hair, I can't help but think
The police get away with so much shit
Oh what's that?
You still haven't found Jill Dando's real killer yet?
Wasn't she the presenter that you all looked up to?
If I was her family I'd be sure to sue you
Then there's that copper that pushed Tomlinson over
How did he admit that and still get away with his murder
And what's this madness about journalist's hacking murdered girls phones
And nobody got jail even when their cover was blown
And don't get me started about that taxi driver prowling the streets
Like a vulnerable people finder he murdered two girls
Then buried their bodies
One set of parents just got lots of pathetic apologies
The other family were lucky enough to get justice
But you'll never touch road
You simply don't deserve this
I hope your nightmares keep you awake for life
It wouldn't even come close to the parents' heartache and sacrifice
In this country it's even hard work to have quiet drink in peace
Without some pissed up teenager trying to knock out your teeth
Do all these issues make me proud to be British
Sometimes I wish I was green and Irish
Arr be Jesus somebody get me far away from these geezers

Daniel Joslin HMP HMP Thameside

Slander, Gnomes And Video Tape

Sorry folks never gonna be committing suicide
Aimee dearest have you got a little spare peroxide
I stumbled through the shadow of death and I'm still alive
If you want unprofessional go Thameside
I'm gonna have plenty of company when I get to them gates of hell
Dan, Pete even that chaplain needs to seek medication to get well
Please Mustafa give me a loan of your fishing rod
Joslin got his transfer, the cheeky little sod
I'm done with Seg. Aladdin's cave is my new cell
Poetry in motion endorses this prisoner to finally tell

Daniel Joslin HMP Rye Hill

Budgie

Smelling like rain
On a duty road
Smiling with eyes
Slightly closed
Singing, when finally
She stops talking
Little legs waddling
When she's walking

On my shoulder
Nibbling my ears
The sweetest kisses
I've had in years
How could you not love
Something so gentle
Without her company
I'd probably go mental

Straight to bed
When I ask
Cleaning up feathers
My daily task
Spending money
On her canteen
Worth it
Just to watch her preen

Landing on my book
When I'm reading
Helping me finish
When I'm eating
The edges of photos
Look like a doily
From bites and holes
And feathers oily

Soft and warm
And full of fun
Green as grass
Yellow as the sun
Eyes sharper
Than a piece of flint
Deep as pools
With a tiny glint

Continued ...

Helps me cope
Through months and years
Feels my sadness
Sees my tears
Unconditional love
My best friend
I'll be with you
Till the end

Tony Joyce HMP Parkhurst

Why Not - or Why

See that guy with personality issues
He's struggling
So what, you say
In fact you nudge a friend, wink and have a laugh
There for the grace of God eh
Ha Ha
Then there's you behind your door
With your own issues
Imagine we all had a crystal ball
And we saw and we laughed
We text our friends and laughed some more
There's a thought
Have a thought
It's just a thought

JS HMP Rye Hill

The Visit

She sat there silent
Five, ten minutes but it feels like forever
The silence slices deep
Cuts like a knife
I look around at anything, anywhere but her
I've let her down again
I want to drop my knees and tell her...
I'm sorry, I'm so so sorry
But my pride stops me
Instead I argue, fight with her, like a stray dog
I'm longing to be stroked but scared to show it
I'm a war horse, I tell myself, I trot alone
Hurt, pain, war, is what I know
Then I look at her

My heart breaks for her
Then I turn my head to slow my expression
I look back at her, she smiles
A smile that lights up a face
That smile, that smile, that beautiful smile
My heart melts
My pride shrinks
I smile

Then again turn to my stubborn face
Trying to keep serious, trying to hide it
On the verge
She taps her foot on my leg
I turn to face her
My face lit up with a smile
Nothing else matters...
Remember that visit?

JSP HMP Lowdham Grange

Charlie And The Letter

Everyone should recycle
Everyone should go green
Some people care
Some people don't
Some recycle, some people won't

Charlie was upset
So he wrote a letter
He hoped by doing this
The world would get better

He put it on the internet
For everyone to read
He used the net because of the speed

Now the world knew how Charlie felt
About the ice caps and how they would melt
About the ozone and the big hole
And how it was up to us all

Charlie had a message he had to send
About our planet
And how it could end

Many people had been displaced
Because of our rubbish
And all of our waste

So try to be good
Try to be better
And think about
Charlie's letter

Mark Kavanagh HMP Buckley Hall

My New Quilt And Pillow

I bought myself a quilt today
It cost an arm and leg
But it don't half look better now
When I make my bed
I really like my quilt
I bought the matching pillow too
Both of them with covers
In my favourite colour blue
I know with my new quilt
I can tuck it in real tight
And with its matching pillow
I'll get a good sleep tonight
Now I won't be itching
Like the blankets make me do
Because I will be wrapped up nice and warm
In a quilt that is brand new

Simon Kay HMP Full Sutton

Cattle

We are herded one by one into moving cubicles
Then rushed off for branding
When the marking is over
We're shoved through a shutter into
An eight by four milking stall with one or two more

Then forced to eat dead brown grass
Which doesn't yield production
That boils up to a cup of oats
Some are then released into a big green field
While others are kept behind to be butchered
And sold for food or compost

Tellah Kinns HMP Littlehey

Coffee And Tobacco

The first thing we mostly do when we awake
Is grab our tobacco
Roll a fat smoke to get the lungs working
Then we flick the switch to boil the kettle
For a nice strong mug of cheap coffee
To clear the circuits to get the brain firing
Then we splash our face to clear the sleep
That collected in our eyes during the night
And to shock the skin into life
We also reach for the remote to watch the news
And to find out what the weather's going to be like today
Then we slug down the bad coffee
And then we roll another fat one and enjoy what's to come
For we are all just simply playing a waiting game
That is life behind bars

Tellah Kinns HMP Littlehey

When I Was A Tikna

When I was a tikna (child)
A wagon was my home
And life was dogs and horses
And country lanes I roam
And hawking elder flowers
Or making willow pegs
Women wore their skirts
That didn't show their legs

When I was a young mush (man)
Then I lived where I might
And life was girls and coursing
And music or a fight
Work was grinding scissors
Or breaking up a car
Old stuffing or the tarmac
Or painting with the tar

When I was newly rummied (married)
In a trailer I did dwell
And I would bill the kenners (houses)
And my mort (woman) would fortunes tell
I watched my children growing
To be men the Romany way
And I didn't know that parliament
Could take it all away

For was I not a travelling mush (man)
Was I not a king
Who owned each sunny morning
Each bird that I heard sing
I could always pick the strawberries
Or course and kill the hare
I'd never have to worry
I'd never have to care

Now that I'm a purro (older)
And on council sites exist
How can I tell my children?
Of all the things they've missed
How can I tell my children?
Now life is cold and drab
Why I gave up all of this
To rent a concrete slab

Kieran Kirk HMP Leicester

The Impressionable Mirror

A mannequin, a blank canvas
For you to adorn and style to your pleasure
Using simple, pure human sympathy at leisure
Such an accessible weapon, as the damage conveys

Quality control check point!
Irregularities leaking out every gaping hole
All that remains is your original goal
You could accept me now, but you don't

Your hands were those of God
I would worship and cleanse your feet
I0 entrusted my life to spare emotional defeat
You'd said you'd make it up to me
Did you think I'd forget?

The water reflect out merging features
Whilst my adolescence is lost
Drowning in a blackened pool as I tossed
Out who I was and my destined future

Incarceration of the soul has not suppressed the mind
I still remember who you were and what you did
To star in your fantasy, of which you never hid
But I was so selfish to want you as exclusively mine

I wanted more of your artificial kindness
More of your infidelity
More of your arrogance and masculinity
More of your empty promises

Poppy Knight HMP Bronzefield

The Departure

Was he lying on his bed
Thinking of the good he did
Seeing angels and doves
Looking down from above
Or was he facing the wall
Trying hard not to recall
Watching demons and crows
Looking up from down below
Could he see a bright light
Not scared of his plight
Could he see only dark
Not yet ready to depart
Maybe for a desolate place
Or a wonderful new home
Where all pain is now erased
By waves of Godly grace
And all sorrow is drowned
By a whirlpool of love

Hugh Kunz HMP Whatton

Where Is He Now

Where is he now?
What does he do?
Is he like me?
Is he like you?
Is his hair black?
Are his eyes blue?
Has he my nose?
A dimple or two
Does he sometimes ask?
Who was his dad?
Tell him the truth?
Or a white lie
Was he my child?
Do you not know?
I would understand?
I wasn't for you
Where is he now?
What does he do?

Hugh Kunz HMP Whatton

Prison Officer

Prison officer why are you so harsh?
My cell mates on a hunger strike, do you care if he starves?

Prison officer I understand you got a bit of power
But officer does it mean you have to be sour?
I ring my door bell and ask for a shower
You say you'll be back in ten minutes
Knowing your break is for an hour

Prison officer why do you want to give me a hard time?
Am very stressed already
I got my court dates playing on my mind

Prison officer I don't want to be violent
You tell me to shut up when I talk
Then say I am mad when I'm silent

Prison officer why's your team tactics to restrain so cruel!
Your officers are like a pack of pub hooligans wanting a brawl

Prison officer just because you served me my food
Does it mean you can treat me bad and talk to me rude

Prison officer there a lot more to say
But I know and you know I'll be here all day
But there's one thing I'll say, the last thing I will write
Your care to inmates, ask yourself is it right

Lamar Broadmoor Hospital

Prison Poetry

I have a question burning on my mind
The answer to this is a needs must I have to find
Was I failed by society and the governed state
Or am I really a master of my own fate
Six years old upwards I was physically and mentally abused, I was no longer me
Now a troubled boy I was labelled with ADHD
Stood there now with my new shiny label
With everyone nodding saying "we knew he was unstable"
Still I try to tell them what's wrong but to no avail
Was this the point in my life I was set up to fail
I tried to tell them it's not ADHD, abuse is the word
The reply I got was your stepdad loves you, stop being absurd
Your family is perfect; they're loving, caring and ever so kind
Your stepdad would hurt you; it's all in your mind
The bruises on your arms and legs are from you messing about
You're family's perfect of the we are in no doubt
If only they had really looked and searched for some proof
All they needed to do was lift the blanket covering the truth
Then maybe I wouldn't have become this crazy violent machine
Who's done nine years now looking at fifteen
Would everything be different if they listened to what I had to say?
Would I be sat at home instead of jail today?
Writing this down I'm still not sure
If I would have turned evil or stayed pure
So I still ask myself was I failed by society and the governed state
Or am I really the master of my own fate?

Paul James Leighton HMP & YOI Doncaster

Oh Joy! It's Summertime

I felt the pipes this morning, the heat was turned down low
And through my picture window, I saw the sunshine glow
I dressed with glee and passion today will be just fine
Filled with joy and baa-lambs
Oh how the sun did shine!

I joined the queue this morning, the usual happy me
The guys all chatted freely, of how their day would be
When Oscar One was ready, we all began our day
Impressed at all the sunshine
But not so of our pay!

Our tutors all were waiting, to greet us at the gate
Though they were busy chatting, and we all had to wait
It's good to know you're wanted, and that people care
Its summertime at Maidstone
Deny it if you dare!

I queued again at lunchtime, to collect my food
When told I was on default, I wasn't even rude
My attitude was positive, I strolled off with my peers
My work was so exciting
It brought me near to tears!

It's summertime at Maidstone, so, evening exercise?
A journey off to Healthcare, should the need arise
Should you fail to grasp it, it measures near to Heaven
Good food, good work, good payment
And off to bed at seven!

Peter Lester HMP Maidstone

Itchy Feet!

Is it normal that my feet bleed?
When they itch so hard I scour them
Scratch so deep my skin peels
They say the feet are the roots of the body
Treat them well and the rest will follow
So I soak and steam, moisturise with cream
I work so long to keep them clean
But am I wrong to be so keen?
Is my sorrow a deeper trouble
Somewhere in the hollow of my aching soul?
Does there bubble up a need
To satisfy dreams of finding true meanings?
The 'why am I?' or 'who did make?'
Am I damned or forsaken?
Left to gnashing teeth of Satan?
Do I hate the path my life has taken?
Should I beg the Lord to bless?
Or just clean my feet less?

Lex HMP Holme House

Probation The Secret To Success

Probation are they friend or are they foe?
Do they give a shit, I'd say no

They come to see me just once a year
We're here to help you they make that clear

It's a funny old thing what they say they will do
If only it was genuine, 100% true

My OASys says I skipped school that makes you mappa two
Your high risk and probation says, do as I say, not as I do

I've had five probation officers now but only met the two
George and Mildred I think, or Lassie and Skippy the bush Kangaroo

I've just read my OASys it's shocked me quite a bit
Like a Gordon Ramsey cook book there's that much shit in it

I guess that answers the question are they friend or foe
Recall Mr Lovell the computer says no

Dean Lovell HMP Holme House

Hot Air

When you told me you loved me I thought it was for life
You promised me one day you would make me your wife
We sealed our love with diamond rings
But I realise now, it didn't mean a thing

Your talk is cheap, it's all hot air
Silence tells me you never really cared

No explanation of what has gone wrong
This silence has lasted far too long
I'm tired of guessing what's in your head
Sick of worrying about who's in your bed

It's not long now till I walk out those gates
The future is there for me to shape
It's time for me to make a new start
Maybe in time I can open my heart

So goodbye and good luck my lover, my mate
Don't try talking, coz it's too little too late

Lucy HMP Askham Grange

Summer Comes

A glut of green
With midge and moth
Awakening.

Pale petals unfold
Where memories of winter
Grow old.

A season bursting
Into fabulous life,
With swallow and swift

Deft and darting
Through a cerulean blue
Agile and daring!

There's a feeling
Of hope and happy harvest,
Of days lived to the fullest.

Butterflies ablaze with colour
Shock the senses
With a canvas beyond care.

Ah, summer comes
Where first we feel warmth
Settle deep in the bones.

Paul Lumsden HMP Greenock

Bang!

Bang bang, bang bang
Is what I hear all day on the wing
Bang bang, bang bang
Is killing my ears and they're starting to sting

Bang bang, bang bang
Go the inmates who are struggling behind their door
Bang bang, bang bang
As the guards march around, footsteps thumping off the floor

The jingling of keys all morning, noon and night
Wondering if I'll get unlocked today for that bit of fresh air and daylight
Bang bang, bang ban
As the footsteps pass my cell
Stuck inside going crazy, tempted to get on the bell

Finally get let out and now free from the cage
Bang bang, bang bang
As I stomp around on exercise like an animal in a mad rage
Association after exercise and oh what a surprise
Bang bang, bang bang
There's the dominoes and phones being slammed down by the guys

Off to the pool table after a quick phone call
Bang bang, bang bang
That's the white, red, yellow and black ball

Association done, getting prepared for some food
Realising its all shit keeps me in a mood
Bang bang, bang bang
Here comes the dinner trolley as it rolls through
Prisoners running around excited as its not feeding time
For us caged animals at the zoo

Bang bang, bang bang
As the grub is slapped on my plate
Preying each day to God that I have many more meals left
Until I walk free out the gate

Bang bang, bang bang
Get used to the noise as it comes with the time
Bang bang, bang bang
That's the punches being landed against the wall in frustration
As I wish I would have never committed the crime...

Bang!

Shane Lynch HMP Pentonville

Pebbles In The Sun

Lobsters mate for life
As do penguins
Pebbles in the sun
Loyalties heat
Coquettish my dear
Fear's defeat
Mysteries explored
Love's meat
Golden eagles swoop
Dancing in the sky
Screeching
Love's whoop
Oh my darling
Lover's dance
Around each other
Flirting
Testing
Boundaries
Love, is a play
Beautiful
Fine
Mated forever
Together for all time
Pebbles in the sun

George Mackay
HMP Frankland

Do Not Pass Go

Clanking keys, cleaning floors
Listening Chaplin, banging doors
Shouting officer, workshop two
Free flow now, nothing to do
Endless tele, hungry sinners
Plastic plates, stodgy dinners
Dangerous days, little pity
Hunting fag butts, convict city
Canteen dealers, selling stuff
Lonely fellas, really tough
Endless lists, shouting guys
Rolling rizlas, sneaky lies
Captive audience, visiting dates
Guilty prisoners, angry mates
Razor wire, massive walls
Family friends, telephone calls
Loving letters, crying tears
Painful feelings, worrying fears
Early release, out by tea
Lucky parole, taxi for me!

Nick Marchant Lane HMP Lewes

From Me To You

Misty recollection of friends
Recalling the good times we had
The night weighs heavily
On my eyelids as I try to sleep

Snowflakes in your hair
Whispering laugh in the wind
I didn't know how deep the river was
And should have stayed away

Tomorrow will bring us
Closer once again
The next chance we have
Could be the best

Stephen Marsh HMP Swaleside

Hidden Reality

The smile is on my mouth
But don't look in my eyes
There is the truth
My spirit is gone

I don't share
I don't tell
I don't speak of me

I listen
I smile
I nod my head too

I keep my cards close
To my chest
So close
Even I can't see

Stephen Marsh
HMP Swaleside

Past, Present And Future...

I see the world in gasps between grey bars
But I recall you in colour even when the dark is heavy
Swallowing tears as though they were wine
As I drink in the memory of our past

I remember your whisper travelling across the moonlight
Now that my ice cold heart has melted away to water
The lilt of your voice as it carries to my ears
And settles on my heart like snow on roses

I stand at the edge of this cliff waiting
Not knowing how it all ends
Craving the delicious future
Like a flame hungers for oxygen

My thoughts are as blurred as a swarm of bees
Feeling as erratic as a hailstorm
But I'll chase the wind until it stops
I'll keep on turning like the potter's wheel

Until you're there again

Stephen Marsh HMP Swaleside

Reality Or Futility?

I live in a fish tank
That is full of weeds, castles and bubbles
But no fish
Or none that can at least be seen
My night-time excursions no longer take me
To places of beauty and love
They are now too distant to even be a part
Of my imaginary world that I have cocooned
Around my fragile soul

It is just concrete and shadow
That now inhabits my cruel
Cold world of reality
My sleep is now as ugly as my day
I wish I could unbreak your heart
As easily as I shattered it when I left you behind
The fever of wondering if this is real or fake
Infringes on my mind each morning
Until the harsh truth becomes normal once again

Is the life we live inside or outside our head?
Is the fantasy within or beyond these walls of hate?
My most fervent wish was to be remembered
As a vision dipped in a sunset
But the grey world of abhorrence
Claims the most tender hearted of folk
And moves them to a place
They don't want to inhabit
But feel they must, just to belong

Only being happy when it rains
Is a painful way to exist
Day by day the steam from the teacup
Becomes more and more invisible
With the memory of lips tenderly embracing
As rain falls upon our love and becomes still
We act and we reflect our hearts desires
An image of our innermost thoughts
Reflected outside our bodies

Step in the labyrinth and discover what is inside
But be sure not to lose your way
Your mind, your future or your desires
The impression of your sleep fills my mind

Continued ...

Marking my pillow many moments after I lift my body
My perpetual surroundings are
Made up of different shades of blackness and darkness
As time crumbles like sand on the shore
Even more so as the silence swallows my thoughts

Since my life has been put on hold
It has been a winding journey of reminiscence
With sinister corridors twisting my vision
But leading nowhere
With their never-ending laughter echoing inside my head
As the laughter receded I realise
It is just the sound of my heart thumping
And yearning for attention
As it reminds me I am still alive

Stephen Marsh HMP Swaleside

The Full Moon

I have kissed your tears
Felt your heart
And searched long and hard
For your soul
But it was like trying to find
A drop of rain in a river
As you buried yourself
Deep beneath your scowl

Our happier times invade my thoughts
And push out the sad
Wishful thinking on my behalf
Remembering the good and not the bad
My favourite times were
Our blissful afternoons
When you made me feel
As if I'd been dipped in sunshine

Knowing that you have the same memories
Makes me relieved
We shared them at the time
And we share them now
Even though we are apart
That sound in your head
Is the fear echoing from your heart
It will subside one day

When we meet again
Under the full moon sky

Stephen Marsh HMP Swaleside

Father's Son

He was the apple of his daddy's eye
In every single way
He looked like him talked like him
When he walked he had his sway
From young age, people judged him
For the things his father done
And you cannot change what's in your blood
He was his father's son
He did not set out to be like him
Still he wore his daddy's shoes
He made the same mistakes as him
And the older that he grew
He too ended up a lonely man
Alone in a empty room
He spent much time in prison cells
Paying for his crimes
They said he was just like his father
The apple of his eye
His mother sat him down to talk
But by then it was just too late
The time had come to be a man
And face up to his fate
Now he spends time by himself
With children he has never seen
Thinking of how life could be like
Or even what might have been
He wished now he had took a different path
Not worn his daddy's clothes
But the rocky road that he walked
Was the path his father chose

Carl Mason HMP Lindholme

Heavy Heart

It's so hard to have a heart
These days
It's getting harder every day
It is so hard to live your life
This way
It is hard is what I say
I look towards the sky
For some much needed inspiration
But it's so hard to find
Some words to say
When all you ever get
In this place
Is just more and more frustration
It's getting harder
Each and every day
It's so hard to have a heart
These days
And when you wear it out
On show
It is easy to get hurt
That way
By the people that you know
It's hard to have a heart
These days
It is hard it is what I say

Carl Mason HMP Lindholme

Moving On

Today is the day
That I move on
Leave you behind
And be strong
Today is the day
That I will forget
Let go of the past
Have no regrets
Today is the day
That I have realised
You never cared at all
It was all just lies
Today is the day
It's a day too late
To change my mind
I will no longer wait
Today is the day
That I let go
Of the girl
I don't even know
Today is the day
You're off my mind
It is the only way
That I will survive
Today is the day
I am not surprised
That loving you
Is just a waste of time
Today is the day
That I'm feeling fine
At the fact
That I know you're not mine
Today is the day
I say goodbye
To the girl
I loved more than life
Today is the day
I love you no more
You can't hurt me anymore

Carl Mason HMP Lindholme

Where Has He Gone

The smell of freshly cut grass
Cold paddling pools
The buzzing of bees
Summer off school
Everything is new
Exploring this place
Jumping through gardens
Nettles on face
The sweet smell of flowers
Butterfly wings
Feeding the ducks
Playing on swings
Staying out late
Bright stars in the sky
Such a small child
With such a big smile
Sitting on kerbs
Ball games in the street
Conquers and marbles
Light nights are a treat
The collecting of apples
Brambles and pear
Mum's gooseberry crumbles
Made with such care
Where has that lad gone
With the smile on his face
You will never find him
He's lost in this place

Carl Mason HMP Moorlands

Reception

Getting to reception is like getting to the moon!
Non-believer of the conspiracy plot
I don't believe it's there. So prove it!
I think reception is imaginary
Though having returned from court, twice
It felt so normal whilst passing through
The 'eye' of the needle
Perhaps 'the staff' are of an alien intelligence
No questions asked no problems given
No trouble caused nothing learnt
Yesterday, rumour had it said
That eighteen 'new recruits' had joined
The list is growing, when will it end
Perhaps when Dartmoor closes
And becomes a 'Hotel' for the wealthy

This second verse has been cut short
The rumour has it reception is 'open'
No one knows the procedure that is needed
To venture forth and be the one to say
'I have taken the first step for mankind'
To reach reception is truly remarkable
To return with property even greater

Stephen Mason HMP Exeter

The 6.20am Door Knock

Rap atap tap, rap atap tap
"Mason, you're wanted at court, 5 minutes"
"Officer, I'm not needed till the 5th"
Today being the 4th
"The sheet tells us you are listed, 5 minutes"
"You're making a mistake, I've got it in writing"
"You're listed, you're going Mason"
On the way to court, it's a day out
I watch the traffic, I watch the fields
I quite forget my circumstances
Then the engine to the van "conks out"
We travel at a snail's pace using, the hard shoulder
"What if we get shunted up the tail?" I ask
"There is procedure, don't fret" come the reply
We reach Gordan Service Station
An hour passes before we get relief
The police officer who arrives, takes complete control
Of a rather arduous situation
We converse and get on like a house a fire
The officer in question has twenty years experience
I was impressed, a strong willed woman
It's not everyone's cup of tea, but it is mine

Stephen Mason HMP Exeter

153

Nae Medication

Ma docutirs took me aff me meds
Nae work the mawra
Fuck the sheds
The only thing tae ease the pain
Is tae buy some smack or even crack cocaine
A fifty send on or a canteen bag
A can feel ma eyelids start tae sag
Al pay it aw oan canteen day
Wae ma shitty jailhouse pay
A couple o halves or some chocolate bars
If a don't stump up there will be wars
The screws are fuckin bams anaw
They put me oan report for smoking blaw
They treat us aw like fuckin tits
And wonder why they get slashed tae bits
Aw we ask is for a wee bit o respect
Surely that's no too hard tae effect
Just treat us like we treat you
And then you'll be a decent screw

Jamie McFadzean HMP Kilmarnock

Gifted

As night time falls, to turn a trick
I pretend I have no fear
And out I go once again
To earn a bag of gear

With no coat on a dim lit street
The ground is full of frost
My inner angel's gone away
I'm a little girl who's lost

God take away this burden
Please just show me light
Don't let me walk these lonely streets
Each and every night

I'm a mother and a daughter
I'm sick of doing jail
God let me put my faith in you
Don't set me up to fail

Bonnie McIntosh Gifted Project

The Viz!

Hooray, hooray you're coming up today
I'm going to see you for an hour or two
But wait, just wait I'm in an awful state
I won't know what to say or what to do

Good grief, good grief I'm trembling like a leaf
I'm scared that you don't love me anymore
My God, my God I'm such a silly sod
Of course you love me darling that's for sure

Come on, come on let all these fears be gone
You're safe coz your sweet lady's by your side
Okay! Okay! She's with me all the way
I hope that I can dream of her tonight

I see, I see it isn't you it's me
My thoughts are playing tricks inside my mind
Oh boy, oh boy! I think ill jump for joy
For you're the greatest love I'll even find

They're late, they're late they've left you at the gate
I pray to God that they will let you in
You're here, you're here I'll just put on my gear
I'm ready now so let the viz begin

McKell HMP Preston

Yesterday Returns

I try to forget what I've done and said
But it keeps squeezing through a crack
It leaks and floods and fills my head
Yesterday keeps coming back

In hindsight I know where I wronged
But foresight, I do seem to lack
To forget it, I have always longed
But yesterday keeps coming back

In my dreams, it seems to stay
And so I dread to hit the sack
I try to push it out by day
But yesterday keeps coming back

I tried to make amends and yet
I failed to keep myself on track
She won't forgive and she won't forget
And yesterday, it seems, is back

James McKnight HMP Dartmoor

HMP Road

Locked up in this place they call jail
Checking the board to see if I've any mail
Walking round the exercise yard
Lots of walking but you don't get far
Standing waiting on the phone
So I can phone my son at home
'Sheds' they shout, I'm off to work
Work all day for a few buck
Feeding time at the zoo
Gotta be fast or its veggie for you
'Check up' they shout, in you go
Locked in your cell for an hour or so
Association 'out you come'
Grab a coffee sit on your bum
Listen to today's jail politics
People chatting talking shit
Jails just like a little town
Whoever thought of it must be a clown
Three meals a day to fill my belly
In my room a flat screen telly
No bills to pay, just £1 a week
Even that people say is steep
En-suite bathroom in my room
CD player to blast my tunes
Asda, Argos and canteen sheets
Are supplied once a week
Clean bedding every day
Oh what a great place I hear you say

Emma Merrilees HMP Edinburgh

Mates Made In Jail

Laid there chillin on my bed in my cell
When my pad mate jumps up and put on the bell
He says he can't handle it no more in HMP
There's stuff going on in his life that no-one can see
He asks for a phone call to his family to keep in touch
It's his first time in prison and it's all too much
He hasn't spoken to them yet and it's left him stressed
If he gets his call it would be a weight lifted off his chest
Boss say no and walks away from the door, he's left annoyed
With the idea of ending his life he has toyed
Boss says he understands it's his first time and it's hard
But no special treatment so he cuts his wrists, it'll leave him scarred
So I jump on the bell, boss, boss he's tried to end it all
It's partly your fault boss, you should have let him have a call
If he dies from his cuts the officers to blame
He says nothing to do with me and walks away with no shame
The screw calls healthcare to see if anything to be done
 I tell him not to do it again, think of how much he loves everyone
Hopefully my words may help him to stay calm
A few days later he's back on the wing with bandages on his arm
He says to me thanks, your words help me stay alive
I tell him to do his best, we all struggle and strive
And that minutes drag but months will fly
Not even the screws can stop the clock ticking by
Months later he's come to my cell and says I saved his life
I tell him you did that yourself I just gave you some advice
A few days later he is released which is great
He was a good lad, I class him as a mate
I receive a letter from him in the mail
He says life is good and hopes to see me when I'm out of jail

Kevin Midgley HMP Forest Bank

This Place Of Woe

In this place of woe and concrete blocks
Our lives are on pause unlike the clocks
Hours, minutes, seconds just ticking away
As for with our liberty we must now pay
Surrounded by steel and razor wire
This place is hell only minus the fire
Bubbling with bravado but not much wisdom
A thousand men trying to beat the system
Two to a cell crammed like sardines
Not my idea of living the dream
But we sit in our cells with just our thoughts
Each resenting the fact that we got caught
Pondering the outcome of our looming fate
Where all we can do is sit and wait
So what can we do until we are free?
Why not tap into your creativity?
Now I don't mean slang for 'having a fight'
But it can feel so good to read and write
There are magical places for you if you look
Get out of this jail and escape in a book
I've been to Venice, Asia and even the Moon
Without ever having to once leave my room
Fought lions and ogres, done missions to Mars
For reading can squeeze you through those bars
Or perhaps you fancy yourself as a poet
You may be a natural and just not know it
However it goes whilst writing your rhyme
I can at least promise it will pass the time
So get off that bed and put pen to paper
Leave the doing nothing until later
Don't use this time to get all frustrated
Take my tip - get educated...

Simon Millea HMP Forest Bank

Not The Canteen

There's a sign on my door saying
NOT THE CANTEEN
Some people think I'm greedy
Some think that I'm mean
But I have a story, please let me tell
Of all the requests when people visit my cell
Have you any:-
Stamps or birthday cards?
Or a tin of custard?
A packet of skins?
Or chocolate muffins?
Any milkshake?
Or yoghurt break?
A matchstick cutter?
Or peanut butter?
A duvet cover?
For my lover?
A pack of noodles?
Or an A4 pad for my doodles?
Any chocolate?
Or coffee mate?
Any peanuts?
Or fag buts?
Anyway gis a few smokes!
And I'll tell you some jokes!
Any razor blades?
Or lemonade?
Baby oil?
Or a bit of foil?
A cup of coffee?
Or any toffee?
Bombay mix?
Or matchsticks?
A bit of glue?
Or TYPHOO?
Body wash?
Or orange squash?
Chocolate éclairs?
Shampoo for my hair?
Any mouthwash?
Or liquid cosh?
Pitted dates?
Biscuits obviously chocolate?
Any cheese?
Or marmite squeeze?

Continued ...

Tomato ketchup?
Or a spare cup?
Now I'm not greedy and I'm not mean
But please understand this is NOT the canteen!
And once in a while it would be nice see a smile
And for you to ask how I'm doing!

Mark Milne HMP Holme House

I Remember William

I remember William, being proud of his new uniform
So proud he almost shone

I remember the way we as a family kept track as best
We could on his exploits in what for us was a far foreign land

I remember when William came home on leave
Changed beyond recognition yet still William

I remember when the hospital discharged him
And he was forever trapped in chair

I remember the way mother was fiercely protective
Of her damaged son living her life for him

I remember taking William out to the local fair
And the reaction to him from the passing people

I remember they shut him away behind tall walls
With the others who gave everything they possessed

I remember that William died before he was thirty looking
Like he was carrying an extra half century on his shoulders

I remember his funeral when others from his regiment
Came to pay their respects to their fallen comrade

Chris Morgans HMP Isle of Wight

I Am

I never knew all that I could be
Maybe I don't even know what I was
But I have time now
The face of time never changes
I must change in facing time
Greet it tenderly as a leaf falling upon my thoughts at night
Unnoticed
Acknowledged only by the silent breeze within me
The moments I knew now
Trail around another's watch
They speak of life's demanding nature
Yet in this darkened space I must demand
More of myself
Forever searching out for the bottom
A point in which to progress
Fingers probe the cavernous doubt
That shrouds my flimsy hopes
Dangling, playfully dancing into eternity like midnight chimes
Silence locks each moment way
Compacted, fossilised
To roar again
Swept up in the changing winds
Caressed into life
Moulded into meaning
And when it flares its ageless arc into the shadows of my mind
Sparking beliefs litmus tail
I will follow
There I'll be
There I always am

J Mullins HMP Brixton

My Heart Is Not Broken

My heart's not broken
It pumps to a beautiful rhythm
My heart awaits a call
Because when I hear you
My heart is in mayhem

My heart is not broken
It longs for your touch
If it was
How could I feel so much?
Your love is so forgiving
If my heart was broken
How could I go on living?

My heart is avian, it whole
It has wings
It belongs to only one
I would not give them broken things

My heart is not broken
Feels like it's going to smash my ribcage
And burst through
Make itself contemporary
And without asking for anything in return
Present itself to you

Some might say
I am a perfidious pathetic pariah
Well on my way to perdition
But my heart is not broken
It beats, it weeps, it never sleeps
Discounts anything said
Only longs for our next confrontation

My heart is not broke
Whenever you are near me
It transforms into a mercurial instrument
And plays a symphony
My heart is in good health
Disregards penury
My hears not broken
It brings me enormous wealth

My hears not broken
Although it probably should be

Continued …

The disappointments the hurt and abuse
Only affect my fragile body
No what matters is safe
It cannot be got to
My heart is not broken
How could it be?
It's being taken care of by you
You are looking after it for me

My hearts not broken
It's not deconstructed
My heart is rooted, established and secure
Although this may seem a mere token
My hearts destiny
Has long been decided

My hearts not broken
Even though I'm sad
It's not solely mine
It belongs to us
I am therefore extremely glad
Being melancholy and gloomy
Is confusingly sensuous

My heart is not broken
Its strong, it's yours and mine
No matter what happens
You, my heart and me
Will transcend time

Lou Napolitano HMP Moorland

Questions

How long has it been?
For how many windswept winters
Has time, for times own sake
Prolonged your non-existence?
How long has it been?

How long has it been?
Do you not know?
Have you not been counting?
Do numbers lose all meaning?
When a sentence has no end?
How long has it been?

How long has it been?
For how many senseless moments
Have you glared into the void?
Is there a reason in your madness?
How long has it been?

How long has it been?
Do you still not know?
Have you not been living?
Do lives not thirst for purpose?
When a sentence has no end?
How long has it been?

How long has it been?
For how many cardboard gangsters
Must you bow for freedoms sake?
Can a tiger tame a tiger?
How long has it been?

How long has it been?
Do you fear to know?
Have you not been looking?
Does beauty turn to ghastly
When a sentence has no end?
How long has it been?

How long has it been?
For how many fickle reasons
Have you knocked upon death's door?
Do you long to cross the threshold?
How long has it been?

Dave Norris HMP Edinburgh

My Preparation

It's eight in the morning, I open my eyes
A smile grows as I realise

The love of my life, my flawless fiancé
I'm giddy inside, our visits today

I get out of bed jump, skip and hop
Excited beyond I'm ready to pop

I've got six hours now, time to prepare
Go see the boys to cut my hair

Brush my teeth, then use Listerine
Repeat twice for extra clean

Then after that, s**t, shower and shave
Go collect my trainers I lent to Dave

Now patiently wait for boss to call
To escort me to the visit hall

Get inside, put on my red bib
Boss shouts out 'table one kid'

Sit down wearing a smile on my face
As all the visits flood the place

Then in she comes, through the door
As I pick my jaw up off the floor

My belly knots, as if Usain Bolts
Are inside me doing somersaults

The moment I look into your eyes
Turning churning butterflies

You know you've got me hypnotised
My love for you fills a million skies

I stop and state the room falls still
Tingles takeover, it's the love warm thrill

My heart beats faster, your looks could kill
So just in case I shall write a will

I try to stand to my feet
You're smoking hot I can feel the heat

My blood is pumping but my knees are weak
I hold you close and kiss your cheek

I sit back down, try to calm
But you've cast your spell and worked your charm

You're cute, you're kind, and you're meant for me
I cannot wait till next visit Sophie

NTB HMP Haverigg

License

Since I have been out on license
It has really made no sense
Not to listen to the horror stories
The recalled cons were telling me
They are constantly calling probation
Saying that most of them are crap
They just want you back in prison
To get you off their back
I have now been out of prison for quite a while
Its very clearly plain to see
All the horror stories I was told
Were not from people like me
If people breach their license
Or try to break the rules
They are going to be recalled
In my opinion, they are fools
I know that it's only a few months
And only time will tell
But to me the license is far superior
To that prison that was hell

So what's it to be
Out on license, or banged up 18 hours a day
Your choice

Ron Nurse

Take The Pain Away

The screw told me today
That my mother passed away
My knees began to buckle
And my head began to sway
Momentarily I went deaf
Coz I couldn't hear a sound
Next thing they were picking me
Up from the ground
They gave me Paracetamol
To take the pain away
You stupid fucking idiot
I soon began to say
They offered me a listener or
Samaritans for advice
What words could they have said to me?
To ease my mum's demise

Leigh O'Connor HMP Bristol

I Had A Dream

I had a dream
My prison menu
Chicken and chips
With all the side bits
Crumble and custard
With a dollop of jam
A nice mug of chocolate
To wash it all down
I had a dream
I had a dream
The moral of my poem
Is
Don't do the crime
And you won't have to
Dream about the menu!

Morgan Octave
HMP Thameside

Dear God

Dear God
In prison I have so many extra things I worry about
They fill my mind every minute of the day
And sometimes much of the night too
God, I find it impossible to get any peace of mind

Dear God
I am not making excuses
But I do need more than just offending behaviour programmes
Yes I am an offender
But I am also a victim of my own gambling addiction
Please God, help people understand
That I need to be helped as well as punished for my sins

Dear God
You know how much time
I spend thinking and worrying about my children
Please God, I am so desperate to get back into their lives

Dear God, I really do want to change
For the sake of my family, my wife
My kids especially - as well as for myself
Is there any hope for me?
God please
Will you help me to turn my back on this life of gambling
That always led me to crime - once and for all?

Dear God, the hardest thing about being in prison is knowing
That I should be with my kids
But then I was stupid enough to get jailed

Dear God, please help my wife
As she looks after our children
Please help her to cope and keep her in good health

Dear God, please keep me strong
I face a very dark future
And please help my family
They are finding it hard
And it may never get any easier
I am sorry that I have also ruined their lives

Dear God, thank you for everything else
I pray for everyone involved in Prison Service
Thank you for giving them strength to look after us

Dear God, thank you

Kenneth Ojo HMP Elmley

Playa

Playas: I just wanna be with you
Make sweet love to you
Taste you, squeeze you
Love you, I can't let you get away
Yeah, that's what they say
Baby; I'm so into you
Where have you been all my life?
But hold on just a minute
You're a playa
You're all the same
I don't have time for your mind games
Cos the moment I give it up
You'll be gone
Running game...

Playas say: I really like you - appreciate you
Your lips like honey
Could I kiss you - I've been longing to
You're one of a kind
Can't wait to make you mine
My love won't hurt you
I've been saving it
For so many lonely days, nights and years
Waiting to encounter you
Excuse me!
Hold up! Wait a minute...
I beg your pardon, Mister
You're a playa
Not the marrying kind
I can see through the charade
Cos I'm not blind... Playas ain't for me... sorry

Maria Oliver HMP Drake Hall

Today Is A Gift

I woke up this morning
Thought about how perfect
God created me
I can't stretch my hands
Blink my eyes
Yawn wide or even a little
Sneeze
Wiggle my toes
Clasp my hands
Drink my morning tea
Taste my Earl Grey tea with bergamot
Life is not about a lot
But making do with the little we've got
My senses of touch, smell, taste
All working perfectly well
I think about how much I have
To give God thanks for
As I get out of my bed
And make my way towards the bathroom door

Maria Oliver HMP East Sutton Park

Life's Path

My life is not worth the life of a villain
If I'm a career criminal, where is my million?
Where is my stash, where are my keys?
Where is my beach hut, the sand and cool breeze?
Am I born to live around violence and thieves?
Am I sworn to allegiance of next man's deeds?
I don't want vengeance but I'm sick of this pain
I'm bored of looking out my window again
Looking at trees and leaves as they fall
Sick of having no credit, hence, no one to call
Where are my family? Am I born upon this?
If a judge was on fire, I wouldn't even waste piss

Because I'm caught in a cycle, too many bad choices
But many more to make
Prison's a never ending session, learning lessons
I'm gonna get myself a weapon, armed with words, what do you reckon?
Forced to face up to the decisions I make
So many paths, which path do I take?

Lee Parker HMP Elmley

Freedom Inside

If I want female company I use a magazine and fantasise
Outside I need materialistic just to catch her eyes
I pay no bills here my toilet is the same room I sleep
Outside I pay for bills every month and week
Fridays I get my canteen delivered to my cell door
Outside if I need something I must walk to the corner store
If I am sick the nurse is always on standby
Outside I must book an appointment and wait for weeks/months to pass by
Prison officers accept and respect me as a crook who sin to win
Outside police officers stop and search me because of the colour of my skin
My mother don't argue with me on the prison phone
Outside she reprimand me for being a criminal staying home
I get fed two times a day
Outside I only eat good when the junkies pay
If I attack my enemy I get relocated to a new prison
Outside after confrontation gun rattle till one stop breathing
The library is two minute walk if I want leisure
Outside I seldom read, money, making got me under pressure
I get to train a lot because me and gym staff have a good relationship
Outside my local gym charges me hundreds of pounds for gym membership
Every day I pray to God and I can feel His presence
Outside I hardly pray nor seek for repentance
Few months left and I am a free man outside
But what have I become if I found a sense of peace inside?

Daniel Parry HMP Dartmoor

Trapped

Trapped within this cage, the bars I made myself
Gone are dreams of happiness, or gaining any wealth
I built it with my anger, ego and my pain
Thinking of myself and always being vain
Slowly brick by brick, the bars and then the door
Lying on my face, spread eagled on the floor
Crying in my hands, blaming all but me
Screaming to The Man, please God let me free
Now I've got the time, to reel back through my life
Seeing all the pain, the struggle and the strife
Gone are all the friends, the mates I had for life
No children left behind, no mother or a wife
So now I look at me, it's never black and white
I cast away the dark and come into the light
I know for me it's too late, I'm trapped within this cage
Gone is all the anger, violence and the rage
For now I sit in peace, knowing I'm to blame
Now I know the truth, I'll never be the same

Jason Peake HMP Altcourse

Dreams

Dreams
Although, they're nowhere to be seen
To dream is my only freedom
And freedom's my only dream
So I 'dream'
Going somewhere so it seems
That I'm somewhere where it's summer
With the someone of my dreams
I'm a dream...
I've done, seen enough of struggling
Seen so much of suffering
Troubles suddenly smothering my dreams...
To somewhere that's so serene
One extreme to the other
I'm somewhere that's in between
When I dream

Anthony C Pearton HMP Coldingley

The Visit

She sits on her own at the back of the bus
He stoical face masking tumult inside
An ordinary mum, she is any of us
"You ok, Mrs P?", "I am fine love" she lied

The gossips made hay. The headlines they blared
"MAD COCAINE-CRAZED MONSTER GETS 17 YEARS"
Her heart was wrung dry, though nobody cared
Not least that crazed monster, the cause of her tears

"A Mother's for life" and "What's done is done"
To awful, trite clichés, a zombie she clings
She waits outside prison to visit her son
And can't comprehend he did all those bad things

An ordinary mum, she is any of us
Who sits on her own at the back of the bus

Stephen Potter HMP Liverpool

Why Use A Little Word
When A Big'un Will Do?

It soothes my soul and warms my heart
To sit and contemplate
Those special words, so seldom heard
That punch above their weight

Like: Funicular, credenza
Vestibule, Pantechnicon
Instead of cable car and sideboard
Porch and large

Pray, why should I say starchy
When farinaceous is quite dandy?
And I prefer concupiscence
Instead of just plain randy

Words make the world we live in
A little more refined
It's good to hear the ordinaire
Politically defined

So make your life more sonorous
With words no smartphone chooses
And describe the day to day stuff
In the language of the muses

Stephen Potter HMP Liverpool

Who Would Be A Politician?

Household DEBTS, casino style BETS
Political posturing, E.U walkout THREATS

Cover ups and SCANDALS, a budget labelled a SHAMBLES
Shadow ministers waiting to attack from different ANGLES

A tax on PASTIES - are the Tories still 'NASTIES'?
Manifesto pledges and policies that are CRAFTY

Aspirers and HOPERS, strivers and VOTERS
Politicians airbrushed on election campaign POSTERS

Pledge after pledge - still no REFERENDUM
If the numbers don't add up - the spin doctors will BEND 'EM

Tories against cops over a word supposedly SAID
"Do you know who I am? Open this gate you PLEB!"

If their rich REDUCE their tax, if it's public PRODUCE the AXE
Just answer the god damn question - stop skirting round the FACTS

Let's cut legal aid - Let's cut the STATE HEALTHCARE
Not to MENTION PENSIONS, EMAs and STATE WELFARE

"We will not increase student fees" - a pledge to secure some VOTES
Another pledge broken - is there really any HOPE

Questions for the tabloids - what's wrong with diverse CULTURES?
Why portray all the poor as benefit scrounging VULTURES?

White Collar Criminals - the reason banks have FAILED
Give me a one word answer - has a single banker been JAILED?

An economic ERUPTION, through fraud, debt and CORRUPTION
Just take a look at Greece - financial self DESTRUCTION

Insider DEALING - houses through the CEILING
"We're all in this together - the economy's started HEALING"

THANKS - MILLIONS - give BANKS BILLIONS
Let the next generation pay today's debts of TRILLIONS

Joseph Powell HMP Northumberland

The Princess And Me

There once was a frog who was handsome and green
He lived in a log near the edge of a stream
He spent all his days the tall grasses among
Watching out for fat flies to flit by his quick tongue
One day when the sun was incredibly high
He noticed a vision come fluttering by
But she was no butterfly skimming the vinery
But a true princess in all her finery
Oh how his heart pounded, he thought it would burst
He longed for her love but, alas, he was cursed
Some nasty old witch had bewitched him at birth
And reduced him to Kermit, for what it was worth
There must be a way to attract her attention
Hang on! There was one thing I really should mention
If he could just get her to kiss him, it might
Lift the horrid spell and then all would be right
But first, just to notice him, that was the task
You would think that it wasn't a biggie to ask
But he obviously couldn't hide in the clover
If she stepped on his head, then the dream would be over
So he hopped on the path and he started to blink
He cried 'Yo there princess! I'm not what you think'
Then he hopped to the left and he hopped to the right
And the princess was taken aback by the sight
As fortune would have it, she had a degree
And had to dissect frogs their workings to see
But, being soft hearted, she wouldn't take part
That is just how it is when you've got a soft heart
So this frog would make up for what went on before
She would make him her pet and heap presents galore
For this lucky amphibian, life would be bliss
Then she picked him up gently and gave him a kiss!
Flash bang! What was happening? The frog burst his skin
And, around the princess, all things started to spin
Then, just as she opened her eyes with a wince
Right there at her feet knelt a tall handsome prince
Still green round the gills, face it, you would be too
If such a huge transformation had happened to you
Then he crawled to his feet and sat down on the log
But the princess cried: 'What have you done to my frog?'
But all in the end turned out just as it should
The pair of them walked hand in hand through the wood
And into a life full of love and blue skies
And, mysteriously, never bothered by flies

Wayne Pugh HMP Frankland

The Great Moon

I look up at wide sky
And I see the great moon
And I wonder how
Why some say it's his doin'
For creating the loon
Peerless sky traveller
Like a torch beam and face
He looks down on land
Sea in from unbounded space

Dean Richard HMP Blantyre House

Homelessness

Listen to this line, when I was seven, eight and nine
My heart was absolutely fine
Now nervy, eighteen on council say not worthy
Left my heart topsy-turvy
Now homeless
Wandering aimlessly without a room
The ever increasing feeling of doom
Sadness and fear in my heart always loom
Alcohol and smack
The love us street tramps lack

So much pain
Walking in the freezing cold rain
All good efforts seem in vain

Dean Richards HMP Blantyre House

My Woman

She's soft and subtle
Always gentle
Smart and sane
When others are mental
She controls her pain
She's so sweet
Little size 5 feet
Her ways tidy and neat
No sorrow coz tomorrow we're together
Always one
Walkin' through various weather

Dean Richards HMP Blantyre House

Bird

Get a grip, deal with it, get over it
Man up, shut up, bang up
Find yourself
Lose yourself
Find yourself again
It will give you something to do
You did the crime now do the time

Find the positives
Plan
Scheme
Devise
Learn
Adapt
Survive
Prepare
They said 'you're not alone'
But you are
So be good company

Dan Ridgewell HMP Northumberland

Lies?

Lies
You're lying
They squirm out of you
Rancid snakes
With poisonous intent
Surrounding my heart

Dan Ridgewell HMP Northumberland

Paranoid In Prison

He tries to think of the times
When she's done him wrong
And he can't because she ain't
It's on the tip of his tongue
To dig deep to discover the truth
It's pointless she's told it
He shouldn't need no proof
She starts to cry you wipe her eyes
You see the signs of strain
Making mountains of molehills
Is the cause of this pain
You need to change
Or soon she will leave
She's been nothing but faithful
But yet you're feeling deceived
Is it the jealousy of her freedom?
While you're locked away
How she walks out from visits
And you have to stay
Nope it's much deeper
Deep down you're annoyed
You always told yourself
You had no need to be paranoid
You need to overcome this
That much is a must
And if not then you're lost
And so is your trust

Rigz HMP Wymott

Free-CAT

To get your attention they scream your name
The spirit needs only whisper to achieve the same
The reason you are here is already behind you
Yet that is all they cling to, to try and define you
If you gaze on this world from a spiritual plane
You would find many amusements in their silly games
Forgive them and the workings of their system
And don't ever allow yourself to think you're a victim
They can wield no power over your divinity
Their societies end, your spirit dines with infinity
Without enforcement their laws would stall
Testimony to the fact that they are not laws at all
The body may be restricted and bound by chains
But the spirit remains free whether wild or tame
Imprisonment only comes with frustration, fear or hate
So forgive them often, forgive their mistakes
Your spirit will grow as you help and serve others
Be guided by love whenever you must meet your brothers
A-cat, B-cat, C-cat, D-cat
Are all irrelevant when you understand Free-cat

Omari Riley HMP Brixton

When My Daddy Went Away

When my daddy went away
My mummy cried for ages
The police looked on with big smiles on their faces

Me and my daddy used to go to lots of flash places
We've been to LA, Disney Land and Las Vegas

Now I only get to go to Leeds and it takes ages
I see my daddy for an hour and in strange places

It's all bricks - metal bars and guards faces
The time goes by so quick
It's like I've been tazered

His dogs miss him so much
It's like they're in cages
I just wish he was home, pulling faces
Making me laugh all the time and packing cases

Dad please come home soon, it's taken ages
And I love you so much
It's never faded.

By Riley to his Dad - Steven Ellis

Identity Struggle

I couldn't help it
I had to look
The address on my birth certificate
Two minute walk from Crane hostel

I thought of her
The affair
Me the result
Her death I'm four again

The place looked ordinary
Suburban
Historical tragedy given
A makeover

Don't know
Whether to
Laugh or cry
Sing or dance

The struggle for identity
Prove
I
Exist

Should take those doubting
Bank job centres
Mother's grave maybe then they
Will believe!

That's if
I
Can
Find it?

Colin Robertson HMP Castle Huntly

Relationship Trilogy

Blind date blind drunk
Beauty intimidator
Whisky enhanced
Sexual hand in glove
Snoring keeps me awake

Morn panic
She seizures epileptically
Awkward dressing nudity
Disconnected conversation embarrasses
Lust's gratification

Maze dawning counters
Night time ease
Chessboard puzzlement refrigerated frigidity
Vertical movement baffles
Lateral blinking

Civil caffeine
Narcissistic nicotine
Two timing toast shares
Shamed shower
Desires departure

Her eyes regret
Reassess
Make a deal
Judas kisses
Promise to keep in clutch.

Fictitious fidelity
Co dependent despondency
Tempestuous temerity
Desirable dexterity
Ravenous insecurity

Beauty eye of the with holder
Habitual caretaker
Entrance dramatic exit stage theft
Plays me like a violin she teaches
Therapy pills keep her serene

Mirror mirror on the fall
Catcher in the sly
Great trepidations

Continued ...

Of vice and den
Insanity spare

Flame haired femme fatale
Obliterates my heart
Marries daddy
Catch her seventeen years hence
Not this time sweetheart!

Princess Barbie my personal tsunami
Private School education public breakdown
remonstrations
Passionately fervent stealing her from Mr
Public Servant
We messed with our heads I hear she's back
from the dead

From coffee society in Melbourne she came
she talked in urbane
Her beauty more skin deep this one I should
keep
The foetal abort while the banks pull a rort
Aware of the riff perhaps we shall split

I picked up a drink time not to think
The banks are to blame drive me insane
Arrested at last now she's part of my past
Getting out in 2005 I'm glad she's alive

Tracked her down in a Psych ward in Sydney
Declared that she missed me
Finally closure happy to have known her
Kerani be okay, keep those arseholes at bay

I find her down memory lane feelings
complain
No agenda or ploy conversation enjoyed
She creeps into my dreams tells me her
schemes
The sun sets I try hard to forget...

The last that I heard she's back on the verve
Cameron defiance attracted to violence
Back on the scene exposing the fiends
Make it this time lives run out after nine.

Colin Robertson HMP Castle Huntly

Will You Ever Forgive Me?

There's so many things I want to tell you
But it's hard to find the words to say
So I'll start by writing it in the form of a poem
And hope that you'll maybe forgive me one day
I knew the moment I laid eyes on you
That me and you were meant to be
We went through so much in life together
I always thought it would be you and me
Things were great, our life was perfect
And we had so many happy times
Then I started abusing the alcohol and drugs
And going out committing stupid crimes
But you always stood by me through thick and thin
And supported me at every court case
You would be sat at the back of the court room
Putting on a smile and such a brave face
But I knew deep down you were fed up of this shit
And your patience were starting to wear thin
But you always gave me chance after chance
Telling me you love me and you'll never give in
Then I messed it all up again
When I went out and got drunk that night
I thought I could take on the world myself
And I kicked off and started a huge fight
I know I was being so stupid
And that fight should never have begun
But when you got involved, I had to protect you
There's no way I was going to run
I do regret it every day, picking up that knife
Sticking it in that mans throat, and nearly taking away his life
There's never a day goes by in my life
When I don't remember that look on your face
Hearing those words when you tell me you hate me
And that I'm such a messed up case
I'm so sorry you had to witness it
But what was I supposed to do?
I know that I took it way too far
But I always said I'd do anything for you!
But I'm paying for it now though
And making the most of it that I can
And now I've lost you, you've moved on
And you're with another man
That's fine by me though as I just want you to be happy
And be all that you can be
All I ask from you baby girl

Continued ...

Is will you ever be able to forgive me?
I've said it before and I'll say it again
I'm so sorry for all my mistakes
Just tell me what to do for you to forgive me
And I'll do whatever it takes

Aaron Robinson HMP Guys Marsh

I'm Fine I Really Am

There is nothing wrong with me
I'm as happy as can be
I have this pain in one knee
And when I'm scared I tend to freeze
My pulse is beating and my blood is thin
But I seem well for the shape I'm in

My teeth are horrid, I want them out
And my diet - I hate to speak about
I'm so overweight and I can't get thin
But I seem well for the shape I'm in

I'm in prison, I can't get out
All I do is scream and shout
My life is a bore locked in behind this door
I can't play the lottery and even win
But I seem well for the shape I'm in

Sleeplessness is every night
In the morning it's no pretty sight
My mind is crazy
I'm in a spin
But I seem well for the shape I'm in

The truth is, as the poem we unfold
That for you and me we all grow old
It's easier to say that I am fine with a grin
Than to let them really know the shape I'm in

Francesca Robinson HMP Downview

Barcode Scenery

Faces everywhere
Pressed against bars
Gasping for air
Like floundering fish
Thrown on land
Like beached whales
Suffocating on sand
Straining to see
The barcode scenery

Blue sky is clear
The sun is high and bright
Yet inside, behind bars
There's not much light
Faces stare out and gaze
At skies marred by bars
Hoping to catch a few sun rays
Straining to see
The barcode scenery

A gull screeches by
High in the sky
Disappears, appears, disappears
A white ball of flickering light
Obscured by metal bars
Only ever half in our sight
Faces peer out at the gull
Eyes listless and dull
Straining to see
The barcode scenery

Bells chime away
Another hour of the day
The church says "another hour!"
Inmates on the fours
Take a moments pause
To look to the far off tower
Hanging out of their barred windows
A wall full of convicted gargoyles
Alas the view is poor
Bar after bar the view spoils
Straining to see
The barcode scenery

Continued ...

Faces everywhere
Dreaming of open skies
Glistening seas
Fields of lush green grass
Forests that stretch miles
And mountains slowly eroded
Dreaming of clear visions
Not ones that have been bar coded
Oh what they'd do for greenery!
Training to see
The barcode scenery ...

Rocky HMP Whatton

Economy

The economy's broken
The system is shot!
Pound sterling's gone down
It's not worth a jot
We hear every day how
Our government has failed
Yet if you want healthy trading
Just get yourself jailed

You can get two bags of coffee
Or half an ounce of burn
All sorts of treats from canteen
Though it'll cost most of what you earn
But there are other commodities
Which you can sell
So follow me round the wing
'coz a bargain or two I smell...

A designer hair cut
Costs only one chocolate bar
That's fifty pence, which on the outside
Would not get you far
True, in here it's a skin head for sure
But outside you wouldn't pass the barber's door!

Yesterday I swapped a razor
For a bag of coffee and some tea
The razor was badly blunted
In fact it was pretty rusty
I was going to throw it anyway
But in here you get nothing for free
So I sold it to a bloke who's rather weird
Maybe he'll look better once he shaves his beard?

You can trade your breakfast pack
For an extra dessert
Just don't mug folk off
You may get hurt...
Go back on your debts
And you're in some trouble
No bailiffs, just a good kicking
Then off to VP Wing at the double

Continued ...

I know a geezer who sells
Great works of art
He does them on boxes from servery
Once he tears them apart
He may be in prison
But he's pretty damn good!
He'll even carve you something
If you can get him the wood
All this he does at a competitive price
Two tins of tuna and some Ambrosia creamed rice

There's lads in the laundry
Who can get you spare kit
It'll cost you half your canteen
But is well worth it
I won some Nike with my highest bid
Almost brand new, only cost me two quid!

The guys on servery
Will get extra food for you
All they ask for this
Is the odd ounce or two
I know someone, a cleaner
Who can get air freshener spray
Though for this service
You'll have to be his bitch for the day...

So the economy may be doomed
On the outside that is
But in here trade has boomed
And the economy lives!

Rocky HMP Whatton

The Boxing Ring Of Life

In the greatest ring that is life
The canvas painted with our blood
You've got to duck, weave and dive
In words as well as with the glove

You must roll with all the punches
Find your rhythm, go with the flow
And whenever you feel he cracks and crunches
Simply give them back, blow for blow!

When a left connects that isn't right
Don't let it beat you down
When your head swims, you lose your sight
Resist the current lest your drown

Your legs are weak, you nearly fall
All you stand upon now uneven ground
As life's shots rock you to the core
Brace yourself, stand tall and proud!

Life is a constant battle, an endless well
Each year twelve rounds to be surmounted
So weather it all till that final bell
Then stay standing and be counted

Because life isn't about never getting knocked down
It doesn't matter who drinks from the victory cup
Life's about surviving, every punishing round
Life's about how often you can get back up

Rocky HMP Ashfield

The Rock Canvas

The sea forms its own patterns on the rock
Which is its canvas
The acidic salt its paint

The rock is hard but feels like putty
I hold it like a weapon
As if - like me - it has been patiently fashioned
By nature over eons
For a deadly purpose
Only now known

Tom Rogers HMP Sudbury

Push And Shove

Been thinking how little I tell you
My heart still smiles in our love
The words lost somewhere
Trampled by feet in the day to day push and shove

It's a tide needs turning sweetness
So much life left to discover
A precious gift to neglect
A chance to find happiness
Within the arms of another

John Ronan HMP Bullingdon

A Taste Of Porridge

What I did I know was wrong
Sixteen months is far too long
Judge don't live in real life
Off on a cruise with his darling wife
I'm strugglin' to pay my leccy bill
He's on the booze, "my man - a refill"

On the road from court to jail
Rock hard seat numbs my tail
Passing my town- there's my house!
Verdict has stunned - quiet as a mouse

Oh my god - I'm in prison
Fingers crossed just a dreamy vision
I'm given a razor - it don't cut beard
Though slices skin just as I feared

Got tattoos so got typecast
No one knows about your past
Gettin' old so lost near sight
Forty years since my last fight

T shirt, joggers, trainers fashion
Miss my babe and all our passion
Economy teabags taste of this
Number 2s (after a piss)

Toilet bowl in swallow mood
Biggest eater of prison food
I keep hair short when in or out
Barber shaved for a quarter snout

At Lewes jail we've got raptors
Locked in, boxed in by our captors
Time it passes and all I say
Wake up fast its groundhog day

To calm my head I lie wishin'
Out at sea enjoying fishin'
Or soaring along high in skies
Hot air balloon silently flies

Norman Stanley Fletcher in my cell?
Nah, another crackhead - welcome to hell

Dave S HMP Lewes

204

Thinking Back

I sit here thinking back to when this nightmare began........
The look on your face, shock and bewilderment
Shouts I made tears rolling down my face
I was in a daze for days
Not eating or sleeping just crying
I'd lost my loved one for eight months to HMP
How was I going to cope, how was you going to cope?

I think back to your first visit..........
I was emotional so were you
I had visions of you being beat up
Because of the soft natured person you are
I was worried if you'd try and take your life
If you had I would have taken mine
Life wouldn't have been worth living without you

It still upsets me till this day
And will do till you're released from HMP
We've pulled through this together
Two are stronger than one
The fight still goes on for many reasons
The twenty two years we've had together
Have helped us fight this nightmare

The nightmare is coming to an end
Not long now babes till we're together
In each other's arms, to cuddle and kiss
Just to touch each other without the rules
I know the road ahead is hard
But we are strong and can do this

Stay focused on the coming days
I was here at the start
And I'll be here at the end
To watch you come through the gates of hell

Sandra - dedicated to her partner at HMP Forest Bank

They Was Ours As Well

We heard the cries and we all felt the pain
One more scar upon our hearts
We knew the cries and tears that fell was not that of one
They was ours as well
We prayed in the hope it would ease the pain
And our prayers drifted like clouds in the wind
Becoming songs from another time with memories of
laughter love and hope
And on this night we all knew
We are not alone

Paul Shimmin Fuchu Prison Tokyo, Japan

Better Future

I'm amazed at the rhymes, I invent during my time
I'm meant to be a criminal
People judge our generation on our clothes automatically 'subliminal'
Poems, lyrics, whatever ya wanna call 'em
Flow so smoothly like water out my pen
I could do this all year long then next year start again

Me and my pad mate sit bored thinking of what to do
So we ordered lots of matchsticks and a bit of PVA Glue
Behind bars nowt but time to keep us entertained
Writing poems, playin' scrabble, amongst other games
We're in jail for acting a fool
Denied bail wish I could rewind back to school
Can't change our past, can't change our culture
Spitting bars in our pad thinking of a better future

Ben Wilson & Simon Reidy HMP Doncaster

Ups And Downs

Recently, I was diagnosed
As having bi-polar
But that's just how it goes
It's something that I live within everyday life
The ups and downs
The pain and the strife
A lifelong struggle with the battle of my mood swings
Affecting what I say and how I act and how I do things
People say I'm different
Some people say I'm odd
But none of them can judge me 'cause none of them are God
I'm in a very dark place
A bottomless pit
I'm always in denial and I never can admit
That it scares me I feel like I'm alone
With nobody to talk to, no numbers I can phone
But then I have my good days when I'm feeling up
I get a boost of confidence and people show me love
The world is underneath me, I'm laughing to myself
If 'mania' was money, you could probably call me 'wealthy'
If you walk in my shoes, you will see that I am bruised
People say 'deluded', but they mean confused
I went to the psychiatrist, but kept getting delayed
He put me on the wrong meds, I'm taking one a day
I still cry on a daily basis
When I'm going through changes
Recognising these faces
The problem with this world is no equality or fairness
I sing this song for you today and hope I raise awareness!

Skem HMYOI Lancaster Farms

Where Was I?

Where was I?
Not in Thailand, in the land of smiles
The distance in time, not measured in miles
Less than a year, more than a day
Less than a mile, but a million miles away
Everyone carrying on living their lives all whilst
I rest my head upon a bed smaller than a child's
Where was I?
Not celebrating with my country, the Queens 60th jubilee
My girl was out with her pal, the Aussie
My friends were all there, someone's missing.... its ME!
Where was I?
Not at my daughter's birthday, she turned nine
Status ambiguous "he's away", daddy's doing time
ABSENTEE, Daddy's only crime
Where was I?
Prison with a load of blokes
Not centre court while Murray held a nation's hopes
Not the outcome Murray sought
A prestigious title can't be bought
A valiant effort, a fight well fought!
Where was I?
Not making babies
With my love, the one I chose from all the ladies
Very much our delight
A clear winner... out of sight
A solitary illuminated light
This was to be her mighty plight!
Where was I?
Not feeling the scorch
At 'V', or carrying the Olympic torch
Watching the Queen of heptathlon, the mighty Jess Ennis
Or the alternative ending for Murray in Olympics Tennis
Along with the Brownlee brothers
And twenty-six others
They stood strong, they stood bold
Together they took Gold!
There was I!
In a cell fit for a mouse
Not shifting boxes or moving house
Bed, TV, toilet, kettle, sink
Table and chair, lots of time to think
My punishment for inflicting a broken jaw
The screws now hold the key to my front door!

D Smart HMP Norwich

An Image So Faint

No bell nor siren mark the morning rise
See bodies clamber in similar disguise
To breakfast call with groans and sighs
My fellow man; not giving a damn

The shadows sauntering about my door
Will return for nighttimes familiar score
For now the daylight rays my floor
The simple things; this routine brings

Each and own, to tethered a date
All men their dreams, their satisfied fate
To walk the paddocks of home, I wait
A looking glass of hours to pass

To mend such a broken scene as this
The forgotten name tags, a mirrored list
Men young and old never truly been kissed
What ink to paint? An image so faint

Andrew Smith HMP Northumberland

Cloud A****AG

I imagine myself as a lone high cloud
Watching blazing sun bake tarmac
And forty prisoners marching circles
Anti-clockwise
But no turning back time
And groups of cons
Like clumps of grass along the fences
Gathering intermittently at cell windows
Where four long shadows fall into gloom
Over pale faces who talk animatingly
Boasting, bartering, buying, borrowing, begging
To gain a different reality of freedom
Pre-gabbs, gabbies, the prison ecstasy
Giving nights out without bars
Mamba!
Potent in its strike
The annihilation strain annihilates
Flips mind-sets then: who cares about bars?
Heart races accelerates, brains swell
Inducing paranoid psychosis
Where bad thoughts dwell
This unrealised deterioration paid for
At prices gone higher than opium!
Subutex
Saliva slick still
Slipped through bars and traded
So where once withdrawal the fear
I float high like a cloud far from here

Jason Smith HMP Featherstone

I Will Go On

I have been talking to myself a lot lately
Paranoia is kicking in and I'm going crazy
I close my eyes talking with no one there
Mind an over-used bungee ready to tear
Falling, fragmenting, crashing on rocks
Too many slammed doors too many damned locks
There's cracks where I once stood strong and tall
Hit me once then twice and like twin towers fall
In this year alone peops that seemed healthy have passed
With weights in my pockets treading water won't last
Fitted up for a cesspit that they call a cell
If my eyes deaden can others tell?
Nineteen years it took to settle a flat
No signatures may relieve me of that
Two times recalled and no crime committed
Police whisper to probation, well and truly fitted!
One year, two, three, see me out on the streets
Woolly hat on floor trying to make ends meet
Or mind totally out there denouncing the system
Because I tried and I tried and still justice's victim

Jason Smith HMP Hewell

Oldest Family Member - The Visit

Aged twelve in a children's home
Loved it!
Three meals, new clothes
And pocket money!

Visited an Aunt not long ago
Asked family history
How surprised I was
When told of mum and her sister
At the same kids home
When they were children too!
What's more amazing is
Two uncles waiting until moonlight
Then finding Aunt Linda
"Shush, go fetch yah sister"
Two uncles stole mum and aunt
Back from social services!

Mum young then, tight lipped now
Never speaks of our past
Nor shows affection
When Aunt Joan held me tight
Stroked my face
Telling me
"You're not a bad person,
Don't go back inside"
I realised I'd missed affection
All my life
Now I reflect
Trying to leave institutions
In the past

Jason Smith HMP Hewell

The Ending

So hard to just let go
Hardy flowers will push through snow
To have felt that love firing dreams
Then watch is separate at the seams
You give it all that you are made
Powerless still, the dream fades
Casual lies accepted rejected
Arrows in hearts so hard ejected
Will bleed and bleed screaming a need
A bleeding hole shut off feed
The delights of love nourishing, known
Deprived of which I am so alone

Jason Smith HMP Hewell

Rainy Association

Crystal droplets, eyelash showers
Nasal drip, drink for flowers
River down my neck
River down my neck

Squelch in my shoe, plop on my head
Snails on the ground, careful where I tread
River down my back
River down my back

Heavenly juice refreshes my spirit
Cleanses my soul, makes me feel with it
River down my legs
River down my legs

Round and round the prisoner goes
Drenched in rain from head to toe
Back to my cell
Back to my cell

Maria Smith HMP Bronzefield

Jekyll And Hyde

I'm Jekyll and I'm Hyde
I've told the truth and I've also lied
I'm happy and I'm sad
I'm good yet also bad
When I'm Jekyll I can be nice and kind
But when I'm Hyde I'm horrible you'll find
When I'm Hyde I look fierce and bad
I smash things about - I'm insane and mad
If Jekyll could always be Jekyll
He'd really feel great and high
But when he's Hyde he's really down
And wishes he could die
But Hyde cannot kill himself - it's always Hyde he'll be
Because both Jekyll and Hyde - they really are me

Richard Smith HMP Ranby

My Recall

Eleven months of freedom, that's how long it took for me
To become complacent, to start taking liberties
Well at least that's what the papers say
The ones for my recall
But truth be told it was only weeks
The start of my downfall

Sometimes I think it meant to be
A matter of my fate
To end up back within these walls
My deeds contemplate
But looking back with hindsight
When preparing for release
Was the seed already sown
Was I destined for defeat

You see it seems so very simple to say 'live life normally'
But when your life's been chaos, to live normally's not free
Somehow when in society
Amongst the rats that race
I never ever settle
Regardless place or face

So uneasy in my own skin, feel the need to medicate
So I swallow lots of medicines and the things I'm taught to hate
Ironic how I hurt myself
To reduce my pain
But tell that t a doctor
I'm just a junkie with no brain

And so the spiral quicken, round and round and down I go
Already tough skin thickens, no emotions left to show
Only a matter of time now
Cos you're living day to day

Actions getting sloppier
Police gonna get that lucky break

And that's all it takes to get ere
Sat cold and lonely with this pen
Now sober filled with pain and shame
I swear 'never again'
And the strongest things I mean it
I don't belong in here

Continued ...

But once again I'm faced
With the possibility of years

So what's the magic answer, is there a medicine
Maybe a cure
I fear not my fellow inmates, but one thing I know for sure
Is that, the answer lies within ourselves
I don't want this for my lot
But keep doing what you've always done
And you'll get what you've always got

James Spokes HMP Bristol

A Response To My Sentence Planning Meeting

How dare you sit in judgement
Of me and what I've done
Please don't think you know me
Most of what you know is wrong

You could find out if you asked
I'd happily sit and talk
But there'll be no questions forthcoming
You don't care what roads I've walked

You won't put yourself in my shoes
And certainly not my socks
I'm just another form to fill
One more tick in a box

To you I'm not an individual
I'm a prisoner stereotype
My fellow cons and I are all one and the same
I wouldn't use your objectivity for my arse to wipe

You want me to do your courses
But don't ask what I actually need
You just spout lots of patronising, supercilious bullshit
It's like speaking to a pint of mead

I know more about non-violence
Than you could ever teach
I taught yoga in South America
My serenity is out of reach

You tell me I should speak to family
That I'm a freak for not having them visit
Is it so inconceivable I prefer it this way
It's not like life 'ud be better with them is it

You don't know my history with them
All the fighting and the tears
The tensions, issues and anxieties
And oh so many fears

I can't help feeling you're unqualified
To say these judgemental, opinionated, close minded things
What experience have you had from behind your desk
Have you even been to the Valley of the Kings?

Continued ...

Have you seen the sunrise over Angkor Wat?
Felt the glory of La Segrada Femilic?
Do you even know where that is?
Or how to pronounce Sevilla?

Were you there when I walked 17k along a beach
And not just for the craic
It was to an Ecuadorian nature reserve
And then I walked it back

You imply I should find it hard in prison
As I'm facing all these years
It's not the hardest thing I've ever done
It's not the biggest of my cares

I survived living with my first wife
I've suffered crippling depression
I've doubted the nature of my own reality
Now THAT was a REAL lesson

I've made a lot of decisions in my life
Some were good and a lot were bad
Some things didn't go to plan
But at the time I was probably mad

Coming here was actually my choice
I did it because I could
Many things I could've decided that day
But I did what I thought I should

I sacrificed more than you could ever know
On that beach outside the temple of Krishna
I highly doubt you could've made that choice
To be that virtuous you can only wish now

There's an irony that's prevalent in my life
It's a story that could be a fable
I feel more comfortable than I did on the out
Inside this prisoner stable

There are more honourable people on my wing
People to whom I'd lend
Then I can count on less than one hand
Who I'd count, on the out, as a friend

Maybe I should've come here years ago
It may've made me happier

Continued …

Analyse and judge that if you want
Does it make me happier?

So, while yes, I did that word
I'm different to everyone else
As they are also different to all my peers
Wasting time in their cells

The prison I'm in is my head
It's a place of my own making
And finally I'm happy to say
I'm no longer faking

I'm living a self-righteous life
I have morals and I have ethics
I allow myself to be myself
And say that three plus three is six

I've had time to read philosophy
My creed it has a name
And having understood that
I'm finding you irrelevant and inane

I could tell you to go read Nietzsche
Follow the way of Tao
Act as if Karma exists
But you would just ask how

I would judge you if I could
And if I did I'm sure I'd find you wanting
For through choice, you don't really know anything
And for that you should be repenting

Jamie Starbuck HMP Long Lartin

Everything I Want To Do Is Illegal

What can you do with an earplug?
Except stick it where is should go
Well one of my fellow prisoners done something
And now they've gone the way of the dodo
Why can't I have a pot plant?
It'd be nice to wake up and see green
"No, that's way too dangerous"
Said the officer, aged nineteen
What do you mean I can't have paintings?
From my six year old nieces
I can't give you that many paper cuts
To cut you into pieces
They're many things I can do with USB
It's a very splendid thing
But if I could do with it what you seem to think I can
I'd be a king
Can I have the internet?
There's no better educational tool
The answer's no of course
 So I sit learning things I knew before I started school
How can it be I can't have?
A colander or a whisk
It's hard to make milk creamy
When with a fork you can't be brisk
Now I don't feel I'm a dangerous person
Despite doing what I did
But even I can see the harm I could do
With a tuna tin lid
I could drop a television on your head
Choke you with a sheet
Blow chilli powder in your eyes for God's sake
Or simply stamp on your feet
All these things I could do
At any time I choose
But surprisingly I don't
I don't even drink booze
Just because one can do something
Doesn't mean one would
Not everybody is the same
Your policy's a dud
If I had an iphone
Underpants and a cape
I'd be able to fly away
But still not want to escape
Not all Asian men are from Pakistan
Not all black guys deal in drugs
So just because I'm a prisoner
Why can't I please have some earplugs?

Jamie Starbuck HMP Long Lartin

Malta, 1986

The scent of a
Geranium; warm sun
On my hands and
Face. Sweet almonds
And ice cream and
The sand gritting
Under my sandals
As I walk into a
Coco-cola
Bar
Coca-cola; ice cubes
Fizzing in my mouth
And throat; click
Of a pool-cue against
The white ball; rumble
Of balls going down
Suddenly
Music
Crying seagull
Voices, and a horn
The smell
Of diesel. Lap
Of the water
Soft and light
Against the wooded
Struts of the dock
People crammed into
A boat as it
Slides out into the
Open sea

Heather Stevenson-Snell HMP Bronzefield

Love Time Rhyme
(dedicated to Jude Sutton)

I lay on my bed time after time
I'm laid here trying... to put love into rhyme

Sometimes I lay for days and for days
I can't think straight, my mind is a haze

So I'll start with my love, that's simple and true
My mind's going crazy, but my heart is with you

I'm a zombie, head's empty, shit what can I say?
It don't take much reckoning... it's my time to pay...

So I'll pay for my wrongs, and for being bad
I've still got you Peaches, so I'm happy and glad

They may push, they may rile, to keep spirits down
What you smiling at Sutton?
You look like a clown

So I smile even more, a reply from the hip
"Don't worry Governor, it's only a trip"

You see Mr Boss Man, to me you're alight
You can't break my spirit and you won't make me fight

I want for nothing, and I'm rich in a way you won't
understand, but I'm going to say...

I've got my fortune, and I will stand tall... see I've got
my two Peaches and my MJ and all
So month after month, I'll do my time
This is my way... this is my LOVE RHYME

Ian Sutton HMP Hull

Unlucky Jim

He grunts and curses, bangs his fist
A scowl upon his face
He utters more profanities
'bout being in this place

He sits alone with fingers brown
You'll always see him with a burn
But there is no roll up in his hand
To satisfy his yearn

Today's the day when all are happy
There is no reason to be sad
Our bags have come, they're filled with stuff
For that we all are glad

"What's up with Jim?"
They come to stand and stare
He loudly tells them where to go
And gives them all a glare

And why, dear Jim, are you upset
And shouting things obscene?
"It's typical of all this lot.
They've screwed up my canteen."

The Little Neutrino HMP Littlehey

225

Prison Is Like My Old Home! Lost

Again sadness had boarded me
My life is like my old house where only memories live
I look like an old man with a fallen beard and dead years
Without illusions, without laments
My eyes fix upon a forgotten port without sea
Nothing
I forgot what day it is today and I don't know the time
Nor do I remember my name
My hear scratches like a beggar's bags
Beating without desire
The birds have stopped singing and they've flown away
But of course if there wasn't even one piece of grain for them
Nothing only sand that moves with the weight of my body
And stones that hurt my bare feet with each of my steps
This is all I find
My life is like my old house
Forgotten
Lost

John Robert Thomas HMP Buckley Hall

On Commercial Road

On Commercial Road where we said our goodbyes
The weather conditions bring tears to my eyes
I wipe them away with my black woolly gloves
And try not to notice we're falling in love

On Commercial Road I'm trying to think this is nothing
Maybe I'm high on charm or maybe it's the drink
The jukebox inside is playing a song
Am I right or am I wrong?

On Commercial Road with the handcuffs behind my back
And the police dragging me to the awaiting riot van
Its then that I realised all I want
Is to be your man

On Commercial Road I see the pain in your eyes
The pain you tried so hard to disguise
Your feeling what I'm thinking
That me and you should be interlinking

So when the say comes that I'm back on Commercial Road
I will put my words and our feelings into action
And let the world know
That we have found true affection

Shane Thompson HMP Ranby

A Lonely Wasted Heart

(dedicated to all wives and sweethearts)

My love has a lonely heart, restless through the night
The draught of evil breath has blown its ugly might
But for a love alone, her despair it must bestow
The sweetest of all sighs upon the midnight pillow
For no true love had ever endured such magnitude of strife
As each and every tear ran the colours from her life
Until a place in time, when first love comes anew
Her lonely, wasted heart must kiss her love adieu

Nick Thorpe HMP Parkhurst

The Coin Toss (Lesson of Life)

You can lead a horse to water, but you can't make him drink
You can educate empty minds, but that doesn't make them think
Life's lessons aren't taught in a classroom, nor in any school
The only way you'll learn them well is by looking like a fool

Follow your heart, not the pack and ask questions along the way
Speak out clearly, though your voice may shake but always have your say
Suffer fools if you like but never look to them for advice
Because if you do, you'll learn at once, never to ask them twice

Respect yourself and have courage in the things you have to do
Learn the meanings of 'want' versus 'need', never mix up the two
Give your support to those in need but refrain from those in want
Your energy is best served on yourself, lest you become gaunt

Live life for each day and for each sunrise and sunset brings
Don't concern yourself too greatly, in the grander scheme of things
The world is built on countless designs and each has its own goal
It rarely fits together well, be sure to make your own hole

If you find yourself speaking, more often than not, sit back down
Or you may find that nobody listened and you became a clown
Accept every point of view, then weigh it up and know the truth
Don't constrain your perspective too much, the folly of those in youth

If you find conviction in a goal, never let it go bad
It's the worst regret to look back and say ' I wish that I had'
Be proud of your efforts, small or not, take strength in what you do
Others may fail to recognise your achievements, but not you

A constant battle to be fought is one of heart versus head
There's no right or wrong, one is a song the other one is said
If ever in doubt, take up a con and decide on a toss
You'll know when the coins in the air, what you want and which side lost

A R Tillyer HMP Littlehey

Illegitimate Sun

Days are merging into night
It's hard to tell the two apart
I let sleep take the sorrows moonlight
To wake again to suns mocking rays

Days don't register as the sun's trail is blazed
Night's veil is thrown over the sun
Fight the thunder thoughts of woe
As once again I'm reared as sorrows son

I awaken to a cloud filled sky
Allowing me a neutral day
No events to emblazon my imagination lit
But the bastard son of a woe is at rest; it sleeps

The torches flare, clarity lit
The forests pathways lead me free
Take up arms of stoic dragons beat
My heart is of a heroes mould

Matthew Tinling HMP Whitemoor

Same Old Song, Different Con

"Please release me let me go, cause I don't love you anymore"

I could not agree more
With these words
Crooned long ago
But prison, if truth be told
I never loved you
My heart? Unsold and cold
If I am to be bold

Castaway as a 26 year old
Feeling anxious, worried
Would I fit or break the mould?

Like a spider spinning a silken web
Justice acted to cocoon and entrap me
Within her monstrous grip
My eyes so blinded and teary
I saw no future for me

But day by day
Year on year
I have learned to cope
And my sanity remains with me
Attracted with a thread-bare rope

The first parole 'knockback'
So hard to take
My anguish coiling
My insides a sibilant snake

So on to Ranby
A new place, new start
So much frustration
Decisions not meant to take to heart

Still have my mind it's in my 'greens' pocket
And my burgeoning hopes?
I keep next to my soul
In an invisible locket
A new day is dawning
A new day has come
A new parole is processing
With an outcome to keep me guessing

I mustn't lose patience
I mustn't lose hope
I mustn't crack under pressure
I must keep hold of
That thread-bare rope

Craig Topping HMP Ranby

Thank You HMP

I pushed her away, my actions, my gob
She took the lot along with my dog
A downward spiral I would skid, can't even see my own kid
Alcohol and drugs a daily must, demonic me, came from dust
Started to get violent, voices in my head
Every copper in the land I wished dead
Certain depression, nowhere to run
Till I hit rock bottom with an axe no fun
Then the police tazer me as a I turn to run
Came around restrained, I wanted them dead
My brain is frazzled inside this head
So here I go to HMP, who gave me treatment
To bring out the real me
I'm not the lunatic drugs brought about
Along with the action of an alcoholic lout
I miss my ex and my child no doubt, it's killed me really
As no contact came about
All I've got is HMP clothes, with twenty one months behind closed doors
Smarten myself up, get education for a job
Gain a little weight, start to look good
Been shipped about a couple of nicks
Probation are a bunch of pricks, they don't want to know my problems
To them I'm thick
But now I'm educated and looking slick
Six months now to a straight release
I feel content and at peace
But all I've got to say is 'Thank You' HMP
Thank you very much for the treatment
That brought out the real me

.

James Trow HMP Leeds

Want Some?

Weed, sputnick, skunk, black
C'mon boys buy this smack
Subby, steds, pregab, hooch
I'll get you hooked I don't care much
I want your burn, clothing too
Do my bird, I'd do it for you
Can get you anything, solvents too
I work in visits, get new drugs too
Maybe black mamba, ketamin too
Want some m-cat, any type of pill
Get you stuff for canteens too
Stuff up lads arses who come in new
A mobile phone, is that for you
All I want is your wage
Do your bird in a daze
You get nothing I get the lot
All for the sake of a bit of pot
My pads rich shower, gels the lot
Even got a Playstation, you've not
You won't get nothing because of people like me
Screws turn a blind eye in this HMP
Lads pee in gloves because they are clean
I pass a piss test, if you know what I mean
I got loads of munches, noodles too
Even chocolate and cereal too
So c'mon lads what do you need
Help me do my time as it's yours I need

James Trow HMP Leeds

Institutionalised

Do you know what I'm sick of this prison life
I'm in jail and I'm feeling institutionalised
This just aint the way I want to live my life
There's more to life and it's about time I realised
Skinnyman you're right I'm in 'prison locked up like an animal'
Round and round we go the feelings mutual
I've got to change my ways because that's kinda crucial
So when I get out I won't be the same old animal
I'm getting too old for this crap I just can't take anymore
Year after year just sat rotting behind a cell door
Just another black kid that failed in society
To prove all my critics wrong is my main priority
To prove to myself that I can be a law abiding citizen
I'll stand up tall and take everyone's god damn criticism
I know I want to change my life and that's my disadvantage
I'll make my family proud of me just wait and see
I'm sorry if along the way I've tarnished my family tree
Grandma I said I'm sorry for everything I put you through
I need to deal with the crap in my head that makes me mad
I ain't a bad person and a definitely wasn't born bad
Just a bit depressed at times unhappy and sad
There's no way that I feel sorry for myself
This shit just took an impact on my mental health
So I'm gonna move on and leave behind this prison life
It's not about being old grey and institutionalised

Carlene Tucker HMP Peterborough

Horses For Three Courses

Like a vein to the brain or a cord down the spine
Grey matter scar tissue all soaking in brine
The next one to die will be baked in a pie
Add the eye lids and kidneys sliced onions and fry
Take the fat and the meat and mince into one
Or dice in small pieces for beef bourguignon
Boil Arkle add Shergar and a drop of Red Rum
How would Bob Champion feel if dished out by his mum
Drink its Claret at Cheltenham poured in the gold cup
Like a bone in your throat in the stall it gets stuck
When it crosses the line it is medium rare
In the butchers or bookies your winnings are there
It won't canter or gallop this cheap cut of meat
But hangs in a window on Kempton's High Street
William Hills is a bistro with a Michelin Star
With a five furlong queue down the road past the Spar
The chance of a table is sixteen to one
Order handicapped Bobs Worth or Frankel odds on
Take the horse to the kitchen and chef to the paddock
In the Kentucky Fried derby I've backed Fanny Craddock
When it wins you are happy if it loses you moan
In the Coral Cup hurdle the favourites T bone
Is it Trigger, Black Beauty or just Mr Ed
Smear thick on Sea Biscuit and call it beef spread
Great days at the races excitement and noise
We ate Clan Royal burgers from A P McCoys
A twelve ounce horse steak served up as your main
And curried Najinsky for a Ginger McCain
There's a Hedge Hunter stew with garlic to season
Or baby back ribs take from Rhyme and Reason
Put the bones in a pot and boil for stock
The special today is smoked Devon Loch
The meats good to firm on Long Shanks and Big Zeb
Try sun dried blue tomato on Comply or Die bread
Our take away service is starting to grow
We deliver to Aintree and as far as Ludlow
Make sure you book early we're in a big demand
For are all weather service laid out on the sand

Jimmy Twamley HMP Manchester

Luck

I kick back and lie in my bunk
Looking at this arched ceiling
I am a boy again

The gap in my door I peer through
Whilst I tie my shoe laces, not for the first time
I am a boy again

I find out I am colour blind in a panoramic style
As I stare through walls as thick as elder oaks
I am a boy again

This ink meanders through thoughts reflective
Pleased, but without a smile
I am a boy again

Mistaken youth now addressed
As walls they tumble like crumbling ruins
I am a boy again

I am a boy again
But now I can look up to the stars

Paul Walmsley HMP Lindholme

Razzamatazz

We come to jail
Write some words
Send them to the 'paper'

Our thoughts or lives
Dreams and woes, maybe
A jaw dropping caper

We call it poetry
Coz it's short and neat
Lick the stamp and seal

Pass it to the S.O
Behind the desk
As he chews his mornin' meal

We sit and wait
For a response
Not knowing what to expect

Our thoughts laid bare
Upon the page
Hoping the 'paper' wont regret

The 'Inside Time'
Postcard arrives
With the customary 'ditty'

Thanks for your poem'
We had loads lately
Automatically, you think 'tough
titty'

So you feel low
Let down and stupid
And decide to put the pen 'to bed'

Only 3 months later
When your 'pad mate' smiles
And says 'you're off you frickin head'

'You're in the paper' he says
'The Inside Time'
'In the poetry section'

'I'm buzzin' for you ya know'
'But just one thing'
'Why didn't I get a mention?'

Paul Walmsley HMP Lindholme

Me, Myself And I

You're a prisoner
Of your own thoughts
You've put yourself
In your own little box
You've cut everyone
Out of your life
You've even had the blade
Of your own knife
When will you learn?
You're just a loser
A good luck charm
For every abuser
No one cares
If you live or die
Your gravestone will read
Me, myself and I.

Carol Wheatley HMP Greenock

The Ten Minute Delay

I never thought ten minutes could ever take this long
The time I'm standing in this queue keeps dragging on and on
I only want to say hello and let her know I'm good
I've spoken to her voicemail more often than I should
I've waited for so long now I've forgotten what to say
I don't have much to talk about, I've been in this queue all day
I'll ring her number one more time
'Cos I miss her dulcet tones
AT LAST I've finally got through
Oh no, 'GET OFF THE PHONE!!!!

Laurence Williams HMP Swansea

Dear John

You know what it's like when you get a Dear John
And your love grows stronger after it's gone
You know, when you were together you should have treated her better
Then you might not have received this letter
But it's too late now; it's come through the door
And the chances are, you won't see her no more
If you were outside things might have been fine
You could have pulled in a club or gone dating online

Now all you've got is a cuddly pillow
So, no more the roses only the willow
But don't feel sorry for yourself, my poor forsaken friend
Look at this as a beginning and not the end
There's a guy on B Wing, I hear someone say
Who's writing to a chick in Holloway
Now, I don't believe in prison romance
But you've got nothing to lose so take the chance
Then write to your ex to tell her what you've done
And that she was just a fling and never the one

Sid Wright HMP The Mount

Poppy Fields

Crying Poppy, why so sad?
All the blood loss, makes me mad!
Fighting, killing, waste of life
Weeping families, widowed wife
Set to live a lonely life
Orphaned children, broken bones
Scattered through vast open fields
Churned up wasteland, home to me
I'm a blood red poppy
Growing where life used to be

Neil Yare HMP North Sea Camp

Imagine

Imagine we're on 'Basic'
It's very hard to do
Sadly here at Parkhurst
That's what it's coming to
Imagine no possessions
Or in cell TV
No kettles or hot water
To make a cup of tea
Imagine only wearing
Second handed clothes
Pants that you're sharing
With someone with a dose
Imagine being banged up
For twenty hours more
Old, infirm, f***ed up
Collapsed on the floor
No help or visiting pal
Cut off from your kin
No time for a phone call
Isn't this a sin?
Imagine no more Governor
With his own little plan
To heap on misery and deprivation
To each and every man
Though staff find it amusing
They will suffer too
This place is imploding
No jobs in a year or two
We'd imagined all us people
Living life as one
Respect trust and empathy
For each and everyone
We'd imagined decent food
And even wages too
Each day no aggravation
And a smile on every screw
We'd imagined this happening
A community as one
The Governor smiles a blessing
On all that we have done
We'd imagined it wasn't broke
So they wouldn't try to fix it
A Governor, a decent bloke
Is as rare as rocking horse shit
We'd imagined that the POA

Continued ...

Still had some backbone
Would they have let this lay?
Or left well alone?
But this new man here
He flouts Prison Law
Cares nothing for our welfare
It sticks in his craw
Hiding behind his desk
His priority is cuts
Never showing his face
He hasn't got the guts
By cutting to the bone
Our facilities and freedom
He thinks he has won
And he'll only have to feed them
But he forgets we have a right
Which will unbalance his accounts
I'd like to see his face
After the compensation amounts
But, the real cost will be a life
It's already heading that way
I hope it ends in the strife
Of a corporate manslaughter claim
So, take head of what I say
Cos everything is true
The prospect of 'Basic Day'
Is coming to a prison near you

Yo Yo HMP Parkhurst

Final Fantasy

This time for us now in ruins because of what I've done
Wasted all the joy I found in you in my pursuit of fun
Blind and selfish thoughts eclipsed all I had or would
Now I'm missing all you brought: soul and body food

Days spent on the couch, I long for those so now
In each other's minds and out, love spilled all around
I miss all we shared, our time in land la la
Do you know how much I cared behind my feeling-phobia?

Now I have the time, I think about our bond
About adventures yours and mine, swords and magic wands
Are you also reminiscing, or is it only me
Dreaming and wishing for one more final fantasy?

Zeb HMP Bullingdon

ISBN 978-0-9562855-0-8   ISBN 978-0-9562855-2-2   ISBN 978-0-9562855-4-6

ISBN 978-0-9562855-6-0   ISBN 978-0-9562855-9-1

Also available to order at a discounted price from
www.insidetime.org - Inside Poetry volumes 1 , 2, 3, 4 and 5